CONTEMPORARY CHRISTIAN COUNSELING

CONTEMPORARY CHRISTIAN COUNSELING

Len Baglow

E. J. DWYER

First published in Australia and New Zealand in 1996
First published in U.S.A., Canada, Ireland, the
United Kingdom and Europe in 1997
by
E.J. Dwyer (Australia) Pty Ltd
Unit 13, Perry Park
33 Maddox Street
Alexandria NSW 2015
Australia
Ph: (02) 9550 2355
Fax: (02) 9519 3218

Copyright © 1996 Len Baglow

This book is copyright. Apart from any fair dealing for the purposes of private study, research, criticism or review, as permitted under the Copyright Act, no part may be reproduced by any process without written permission. Inquiries should be addressed to the publisher.

National Library of Australia
Cataloguing-in-Publication data

> Baglow, Len, 1956-.
> Contemporary Christian counseling.
>
> Includes index.
> ISBN 0 85574 302 6.
>
> 1. Pastoral counseling. 2. Counseling. 3. Spiritual direction. 4. Caring - Religious aspects - Christianity.
> I. Title.
> 253.5

Cover design by Mango Design Group
Text design by Mango Design Group
Typeset in 12pt Sabon by Adept Type Pty Ltd
Printed in Australia by Griffin Paperbacks

10 9 8 7 6 5 4 3 2 1
00 99 98 97 96

Distributed in the United States by:
  Morehouse Publishing
  PO Box 1321
  HARRISBURG PA 17105
  Ph: (1800) 877 0012
  Fax: (717) 541 8128

Distributed in Ireland and the UK by:
  Columba Book Service
  55A Spruce Avenue
  Stillorgan Industrial Park
  BLACKROCK CO. DUBLIN
  Ph: (01) 294 2556
  Fax: (01) 294 2564

Distributed in Canada by:
  Novalis
  49 Front Street East
  Second Floor
  TORONTO, ONT M5E 1B3
  Ph: (1800) 387 7164
  Fax: (416) 363 9409

Distributed in New Zealand by:
  Catholic Suppliers (NZ) Ltd
  80 Adelaide Road
  WELLINGTON
  Ph: (04) 384 3665
  Fax: (04) 384 3663

Acknowledgments

This book would not have been possible without the assistance and encouragement of many people. It is hard to overemphasize the influence of Sandra Sewell. She has been both gentle encourager and relentless critic. I would also like to thank Stanley Hauerwas and his friend Logan Jones who have so kindly given of their time to help a "bloke on Bribie Island." Anne Dawson OSU helped greatly with the preparation of Chapter Two, and indirectly Anne's influence may be found throughout the book. Neil Ormerod made helpful comments when the book was in early draft form and Ormond Rush gave similarly helpful comment when it was almost finished.

My wife Sue was supportive throughout even when the rigors of writing made me somewhat distracted. My daughter Fiona constantly brought me back to reality.

Finally I gratefully acknowledge permission for the use of the following material:

Extracts from *The Truth Shall Make You Free* by Gustavo Gutiérrez, Orbis Books, Maryknoll, N.Y., 1990.

Extracts from "Just Call Me Arch" by Anuradha Vittachi, *The New Internationalist* (July 1992, p.35).

Growing Together, © 1973 by George and Donni Betts. Reprinted by permission of Celestial Arts, Berkeley, CA.

Tears and Pebbles in My Pockets, © 1976 by George Betts. Reprinted by permission of Celestial Arts, Berkeley, CA.

Unless otherwise indicated, the scriptural quotations are from the *Jerusalem Bible*, © 1966 by Darton, Longman and Todd Ltd. and Doubleday, a division of Bantam Doubleday Dell Publishing House, Inc.

Contents

1. Christian Counseling: Beginnings, Definitions and Dilemmas — 1

2. Counseling and God's Providence: Liberation to Love — 11

3. Love and Freedom: Integral to Christian Counseling — 23

4. Growing in Faith and Love — 35

5. Analysis and Conversion — 51

6. Practice Application: Counseling and Child Abuse — 65

7. Christian Theology and Understanding of Methods of Counseling — 83

8. The Church as Sign of Liberation — 97

Index — 114

Christian Counseling: Beginnings, Definitions and Dilemmas

THE NEED FOR INTEGRATION

Many Christians become counselors. Once having taken on the role, we can discover that counseling presents many dilemmas. These dilemmas cluster round three main issues i.e. aims, methods and consequences. It is important for Christians to have a framework within which to think about and be critical of their work, for without such a framework they will quickly find themselves engaged in practices that are both counter-productive to the good of those who seek help, and counter to the good news that is implicit in all Christian lives.

The purpose of this book is to offer a synthesis of recent Christian theology and counseling practice and so assist the Christian practitioner (or student) to construct or clarify a framework for practice. The task is not without difficulties, chief of which might be signaled by the question, "Why bother?" For many people today, questions of theology seem peripheral. We live in an age and in a society that does not take God into practical account in the daily matters of living. By and large, religion is either a matter of private feeling and belief, or the temporal power associated with the institutional church. Or it may be a vague theism that supports "niceness," while being deeply ambivalent about religion, yet at the same time hedging its bets and investing in what might well be termed an inter-terrestrial insurance policy.

Yet if, as Christians believe, God created the world, and saved it, and sent the Spirit of God to be among us, theology is very much about reality, and it is intellectually dishonest to construct ways of thinking about the world that exclude God. By the same argument, all Christian actions should be informed by an awareness of God as part of daily reality.

It is a responsibility of the Christian counselor, as in other aspects of life, to do God's will as he or she understands it. In the counseling relationship, this responsibility means that it is not good enough for the Christian counselor to compartmentalize Christianity and counseling. Christianity is not a private matter, as the secular state would have us at times believe. The more authentic Christianity is, the more it transforms every aspect of a Christian's life. The Christian counselor who does not inform counseling practice with consistent theological reflection develops an inconsistent practice which is of dubious use to counselees and which erodes the integrity of the counselor.

The attempt to achieve integration is also not without its difficulties. Trained initially as a social worker in the humanist tradition, I am aware that my own attempt to integrate religion with counseling may well be regarded with suspicion. Likewise, the pastor or priest or other committed Christian who is involved in counseling tends to be regarded by counseling professionals as an eccentric amateur: the most that can be expected is that he/she gives a bit of moral support and does no harm. Similarly, of course, professional counselors are often regarded by many in the churches as incompetent theorists — too abstract, too young or too silly — who never address the "real" spiritual and moral issues with which people grapple.

It is my belief that both sides miss out in this standoff. Professional counselors can miss out when they fail to take seriously a counselee's own constructed system of meaning discounting the wisdom of the Christian tradition that has been a part of Western culture for two thousand years, and which, despite reports to the contrary, is still a potent force in many individual lives and in society as a whole. Religious counselors, too, miss out because their theology, by and large, has not responded adequately to the modern age and has found itself somewhat peripheral to the main advances in counseling this century. I would argue, therefore, that there is much to be gained by developing a Christian theology of counseling that speaks to our experience as counselors in the last part of the twentieth century.

COUNSELING: DEFINITIONS AND DESCRIPTIONS

When I first began to look into the theology of counseling, I found I needed to explore the world of pastoral counseling. In trying to explain pastoral counseling, William Hulme has argued that: "The uniqueness of pastoral care and counseling is focused on the meaning of the word pastoral. The title pastor carries a symbolic role with a long tradition."[1] For Hulme, a pastor is primarily an ordained minister, and the authority to counsel is based on ordination. Hulme's view appears to be commonly held in the pastoral counseling literature, though it is not the only opinion. Certainly this view caused me some consternation as I began to study the literature, an experience not unlike stepping through Alice's looking glass. The basic geography of the counseling world, the terrain I knew from social work and from interdisciplinary practice, still seemed the same, but many of the roles, actions and expectations of the players seemed different. This was epitomized for me in an article by Richard Vaughan entitled "Lay Persons as Pastoral Counselors."[2] In the opening sentence, Vaughan states: "Up until recently, the ministry of pastoral counseling was the exclusive prerogative of priests, a practice dating back to the early fathers of the church."[3] This was certainly news to me. Here was a parallel world and one to which, for example, women were only lately admitted, whereas in my world they had long been the backbone of the profession, and indeed the founders. According to Fr. Vaughan, pastoral counseling "is a dialogue between a person who represents a church and a member of that church."[4] This explains his requirement that pastoral counselors "not only know what the church teaches but that they believe it and put it into practice."[5] In Fr. Vaughan's article pastoral counseling has a narrow institutional function, and it would be hard to imagine Fr. Vaughan having anything meaningful to say to a person who was not of the same denomination.

The church established by Christ is larger than any one denomination, and I know of no one who can tell me where its boundaries lie. Every church member represents the church, and therefore has a potential role to play in the faith development, personal development and the resolution of problems that are a part of counseling, pastoral or otherwise. Though the tradition of pastoral counseling has some important insights to offer the Christian counselor, for me it also has a number of important shortcomings.

These shortcomings arise not so much because the pastoral tradition has narrowed the concept of counseling, but more importantly because the tradition has misconceived the church. Pastoral counselors have tended to take as orthodox, or proper, that which was their practice — i.e. the vesting in their ordained ministers of the gift, charism, art and science of counseling — leaving unexamined not only their ordination policy, but also only half examined the relationship between ministry and counseling. When the question arises of how the theology of counseling is related to actual counseling in the world, pastoral counselors are often left floundering. When an institutional model of the church predominates, it is hard to build connections with the social sciences, and to the world in general, in other than a superficial, mechanistic or functional manner. Techniques of counseling and techniques of religion tend to be tacked together in an uncomfortable alliance. This is not to say that a deal of good counseling work is not done, judging by the sensitive and often brilliant descriptions of pastoral work. However, pastoral counselors have, by and large, failed to describe adequately what it means to be a Christian and a counselor.

I felt I needed to go beyond the insights of the pastoral counselors, while appreciating much of the benefit that they have to offer. In this "going beyond," I have found the work of the theologian, Gustavo Gutiérrez, particularly useful. Gutiérrez has sought to engage, in various ways, in a theological dialogue with the social sciences at the level of practice and activity. This added dimension is, to me, important, for counseling is more than a social science. It is the living practice of all kinds of counselors who seek to bring about personal and social change. In their practice, counselors are variously influenced by the social sciences that provide a backdrop, both formal and informal, to their work. Practice, however, continually stretches the existing boundaries of the social sciences, deepening the knowledge base of social science and making new discoveries in the very act of counseling. At its best, counseling can transcend the confines of social sciences, and become art.

When we consider professional counseling, we find that in Western society there is a relatively large group of people who earn part or all of their living from the giving of counsel. Such people include psychiatrists, psychologists, social workers, occupational therapists, family therapists and pastoral counselors, to name but a few. There are also a wide variety of counseling techniques — psychoanalysis, psychotherapy, client centered therapy, gestalt and many others. Such variety reflects both the diversity of people's needs, and the divergency of possible responses, in times of great change and in societies characterized by cultural diversity. Counseling sessions may consist of one short session with a counselor, or may continue regularly and intensively, or irregularly, for many years. People may seek to solve relatively minor emotional, social or psychological problems (say, in response to a transitory event like a robbery), or they may set out to solve complicated and deeply embedded problems such as long-standing personality problems.

Beyond formal counseling, in which one party has a relatively stable role of counselor and the other of counselee, there is also informal counseling that takes place between friends and sometimes acquaintances. These counselors may have very little formal status, for example, the wise neighbor who is a source of wisdom and assistance to the neighborhood, but such people are invaluable to the cohesion and cooperation of communities of people. They have probably always existed, yet they have not, by and large, come to the attention of official historians, perhaps because they have often been women.

COUNSELING IN CONTEXT: TIME, CLASS, SOCIETY, CULTURE AND WORLD EVENTS.

Counseling is not simply about helping individuals or families in isolation; it is also about helping them in the context of the society and the time in which they live. The nature of counseling has changed substantially this century along with the societies of individuals it serves. Those of us who have grown up in the twentieth century cannot escape the influence of the great theoreticians and thinkers of our age such as Freud, Jung, Watson, Skinner and Piaget, even if we do not agree with their theories. Many problems have been defined in medical terms that might previously have been defined socially, morally or religiously. Issues of authority and status have also changed.

A medieval person would have expected to be counseled by someone with authority confirmed by office (e.g. a priest/ bishop with the authority of holy orders) or status (e.g. a young man of the knightly class might be counseled by an older man.)[6] Though medieval counseling was quite different from that which we experience today, there are surprising similarities. Pastoral counseling and the tradition that the authority of the counselor comes from the ministerial role, has a long history. The other locus of authority, status, is still important in counseling. We see this in the bureaucratization of counseling, and the state's employment of counselors who accrue at least some status from being employees of the state. Status can vary according to the counselor's employing body. Hence, a counselor employed by a university may have higher perceived public status than one employed by a low profile welfare body.

Professionalization is another contributing factor to perceived status and authority. Professionalization is a complex phenomenon. Greenwood claims that all professions possess five distinguishing attributes: systematic theory, authority, community sanction, ethical codes and a culture.[7] While no one professional group has laid claim to the whole of the counseling field, various professions have laid claim to parts as being within their own particular field of competence. At one level, the professionalization of counseling is about improving quality and maintaining standards. At another level, it is about the protection of powers and privileges which are enjoyed by professional groups and the class to which they belong. It is part of the mythology of most professional groups that the protection of powers and privileges is synonymous with the protection of standards. However, the relationship between the two is far from clear cut. While the professionalization of aspects of counseling has undoubtedly improved standards, the process at times has also led to greater conservatism amongst counselors and reluctance to engage in controversial societal problems that may damage professional prestige and threaten privileges.

Growing professionalization may, in fact, be one of the reasons why contemporary counselors have often emphasized intrapsychic and intrafamily characteristics and dynamics, and ignored or have left unaccounted major societal trends. The twentieth century has been marked by tremendous changes, including a huge growth in our knowledge about the world and our influence over it, particularly by means of the expanding power of technology. Though beneficial for some, the changes of this century have brought great dislocation and pain to many others. There are a number of major events that have seriously affected large percentages of the population in their ability to live fulfilled lives. These events have included the continuing dispossession of indigenous people of their lands; the First and the Second World Wars (including the widespread bombing of civilian targets and the use of the atom bomb); the use of concentration camps and torture; migration; unemployment and poverty; the encouragement of addictive drugs, particularly alcohol and tobacco; the prevalence of child abuse; the unwanted effects of technical progress, e.g. pollution and the road toll; the subjugation of the media so that it becomes an agent of propaganda; and the emphasis on material success and technical cleverness, rather than on the growth of wisdom.

These and similar events have so coalesced in our society that no aspect of our culture, nor any individual, can escape them. This logjam of events has crippled hope, and we see in many people a tendency towards sterility in their intellectual, imaginative, ethical, political and spiritual lives. Many of us spend more and more effort defending ourselves against unpleasant realities. We avoid, we deny and we take flight into fantasy. An understanding of the social context of counseling needs to take into consideration this wider reality that limits so many individual lives.

Christians need to be open to the possibility that our society, in its rejection and distortion of the good news, is itself deviant and the source of many individual and personal problems that are in need of solution. Christians have the benefit not only of social and structural analysis but also of a whole world view: it is not just the individual who needs saving, but the world itself. There is a role for the Christian counselor to be someone who can address not just the individual or family, but also the imperfect and often oppressive society in which those people live. In this way, the role of counselor and prophet may at times overlap.

In this chapter I have defined counseling broadly and, by this definition, most people could at some time in their lives be described as counselors. This broad definition of counseling, I believe, reflects people's subjective experiences of mutuality and caring with others and their attempts from time to time to help one another in ways that go beyond the simply material. Every Christian who offers such help experiences some of the dilemmas of the counseling role, such as: "What are my aims? How am I to relate in this role? What happens when my own values and preconceptions are challenged?" In order for us to address these dilemmas, we need to discern God's will with regard to counseling. This discernment is a central concern of the next chapter and, indeed, a central theme of the book.

---

[1] Hulme, William E., *Pastoral Care and Counseling: Using the Unique Resources of the Christian Tradition,* Augsburg Publishing House, Minneapolis, 1981, p.13.
[2] Vaughan, R. P., "Lay Persons as Pastoral Counselors," *Human Development,* Vol.9, No.4, pp.33-37.
[3] ibid, p.33.
[4] ibid, pp.33-34.
[5] ibid, p.34.
[6] Kennedy, Michael J., Lecture in Medieval History, University of Glasgow, "*Personal Communication,*" Glasgow, 12 July, 1992.
[7] Greenwood, Ernest, "Attributes of a Profession," in Mayer N. Zald, [ed.] *Social Welfare Institutions: A Sociological Reader,* John Wiley and Sons Inc., New York, 1979, p.510.

Counseling and God's Providence: Liberation to Love

HUMAN BEINGS AND DIVINE WILL

It might seem audacious to ask the question, "How is counseling a part of God's will for the world?" How are we to know the mind of God? Yet it is the profound belief of the Christian community that God is a God of loving self-revelation. God's will is revealed by actions in our history and in our lives. Indeed, there is no meaningful Christian action unless that human action is linked to the Divine will, or, as it is sometimes called, God's providence.

Divine providence has at times been understood very narrowly, which has led to a great deal of unfortunate confusion. There has been a tendency in some Christian circles to think of God's providence as a cosmic blueprint, or map, which is knowable in detail and into which our actions do or do not fit. On this understanding, if our actions fit, then well and good; if they don't, then we are doomed, and we fall off the edge of the map, so to speak. I believe that this is a particularly inadequate, limited and impersonal way of thinking about God's providence. When I use the term "God's providence," I am envisaging a much more personal and interactional process. Providence is a free, loving action of God that aims to call humans and, indeed, all of the universe into a right relationship, a relationship of intense and deepening love. Human beings, in so far as they respond positively to God's providential call, enter more deeply into the fabric of God's providence. God's action and the person's action become one. In so far as persons react negatively, with an absence of love, and seek to act outside God's providence, God's loving action is inhibited, with painful consequences both for the person and the rest of creation. Such actions cause a separation from the God who is, ultimately, our true destiny and life itself.

Thankfully, however, there is always the opportunity, even God's desire, that the person is invited to be part of God's providential action again. God's providence is constantly alert to human action and aspiration, so that at any moment the person is free to choose life. When someone has been lost to life and returns to living and loving, it seems that God's love is ecstatic and celebratory. Hence, in the parable of the prodigal son, the father is described as being moved by pity for his son, running to the boy, clasping him in his arms, kissing him tenderly, ordering that a robe be placed on his back, a ring on his finger, sandals on his feet, and that the fatted calf be killed. Then the boy's father prepares a celebration. (Luke 15:20-24) This joyous celebration of the return to life from being lost is also the conclusion of the parables of the lost sheep and the lost drachma. (Luke 15:4-10)

With the coming of Jesus in human history, the extraordinary depths of God's commitment to humans and to the world in which they live is revealed. Jesus, the one who is both God and God's son, takes upon himself all the sin, pain and hurt that we, in rejecting God's providence, have created. Similarly, the sending of the Holy Spirit is a further expression of God's providence. God's providence, then, is constantly new, though its core intention — God's call to a deeper and more loving relationship — remains unchanged. These providential acts of God in history are, for those who accept them, salvation.

The scriptures are the stories of this unfolding salvation history, God's great providential acts in history and culture. In the scripture we find images of God the Creator and Divine Planner; God the Liberator; God as Wisdom; the Incarnated Christ; and the Holy Spirit at work in the church which is the Body of Christ. As well as through the words of scripture, God's action is also partially discernible through reflection on the world, the creation of God, in which the cosmic/incarnate Christ is present and through which the power of the Holy Spirit flows. This is the world in which we, as counselors, enter into a relationship with the mysterious "other," both counselee and God. In what follows here, both scripture and reflection on the world will help us gain a clearer picture of how counseling can be a part of God's providence. We turn first to scripture to explore various descriptions and images of the counselor and the activity of counseling.

GOD AS COUNSELOR IN THE OLD TESTAMENT

Throughout scripture we find an image of a God who is intimately involved in the welfare of people. In the Old Testament, God is perceived as being primarily concerned with the chosen people, the Jews. Gradually, it becomes apparent that God's self-revelation is for all. What is more, this self-revelation is primarily about the relationship between God and people. The Covenants, both Old and New, are fundamentally concerned with an ever deepening love relationship, and in every book of scripture we can gain insights into this ongoing relationship.

God's counsel calls and frees the people to participate in the Divine loving relationship of what we have, ultimately, come to call the Trinity. Righteousness is to live this relationship. God's counsel frees the person from the limitations of human folly and injustice, and continually allows for a new start — most powerfully expressed in the prophetic poem of Isaiah (9:1-7), in which God is described as:

> Wonder-Counselor, Mighty-God,
> Eternal-Father, Prince-of-Peace.

In Isaiah's poem, God is the primary counselor of the people, and out of this relationship springs everything that is good, and all that people need: darkness banished; increase of joy; the certainty of justice; and an end to warfare. A new order is established, based on the love of Yahweh. Mysteriously, the new order is brought about by the birth of a child, which later Christians were to interpret as the birth of Jesus.

In the Old Testament, God is not restricted to giving counsel directly, as occurred when Moses received the law in the desert. It is more common for God's counsel to be channeled through human beings, often through a prophet. Similarly, scriptural counselors, despite their various historical manifestations — whether they are counseling kings or people, whether they are encouraging or criticizing — are expected, as good counselors, to interpret God's providence in their historical situation. Good counseling is a blessing from God, a manifestation of the love and faithfulness of God, the supreme counselor, who established the original creation and whose providence is ongoing. It is, therefore, God who ultimately interprets God's providence for humankind, and the counselor who transmits this message. It follows that no one can counsel God. It follows, too, that counseling is worthless, even dangerous and condemned, outside this interpretive, relational process between God and God's people. (Is 29:15-30:5)

There is also in scripture a growth in association between Wisdom and counsel. Good counsel becomes a function of Wisdom.

> In Proverbs (8:12-14), Wisdom speaks:
> I, Wisdom, am mistress of discretion,
> the inventor of lucidity of thought.
> Good advice and sound judgement belong to me,
> perception to me, strength to me.

However, the association of counsel with Wisdom heightens a tension that we noted at the beginning of this chapter. How can humans hope to discern and announce the counsel of God? Job, in responding to Yahweh, exclaims:

> You ask: Who is this obscuring counsel yet lacking knowledge?
> But I have spoken of things which I have not understood,
> things too wonderful for me to know.
> (Job 42:3) (REB)

Deutero-Isaiah has previously complained in another context, but prophetically, that there is no counselor capable of responding to the bearer of good news to Jerusalem (Is 41:28), and the writer of the Proverbs makes the comment that even in human affairs:

> Counsel in another's heart is like deep water,

The author then concludes with an apparent disclaimer:

> but a discerning person will draw it up. (Prv 20:5) (REB)

Herein lies a paradox. On the one hand, human purposes are deep and difficult to probe: on the other, the writer suggests with great confidence, that the discerning person has only to draw them out.

We have, then, two paradoxes: firstly, God's counsel is a gift, yet God's ways are unknowable; secondly, while understanding the other person is extremely difficult, it is, for the discerning, a straightforward matter.

THE NEW TESTAMENT: JESUS AND THE HOLY SPIRIT AS COUNSELOR

It is with the coming of Jesus that the first of these paradoxes is resolved. Jesus is God's self-revelation made concrete. God remains unknowable, but God comes in a form even little children can understand.

Though not described specifically as a counselor, it is clear that in his life Jesus saw himself as part of the ongoing counseling process between God and people. Jesus is both the Counsel (the Way, the Truth and the Life) and the Counselor (the Spirit of the Lord has been given to me – Luke 4:18). He sees and addresses the hidden thoughts and feelings of those about him. (Luke 9:46-48) He speaks God's message of good news both to individuals and to the people as a whole. Jesus is God, and yet he so identifies with those whom he counsels that he becomes human, sharing the common life, and even accepting death on a cross. He thus takes upon himself freely the consequences of humankind's failure to heed the counsel of God. He does this so that all creation can be freed from the terrible effects of humankind's rebellion.

While an understanding of Jesus is therefore pivotal to an understanding of the role of Christian counselor, yet Christian counseling is much more than a replication of what the person Jesus did. Rather, it is the counselor's participation in that ongoing work, and Jesus by his person, both as God and man, which makes this possible.

Following Jesus' death and resurrection, there is the sending of the Holy Spirit. This is promised in the gospel of John:

> I shall ask the Father,
> and he will give you another Advocate
> to be with you forever,
> that Spirit of truth
> whom the world can never receive
> since it neither sees nor knows him:
> but you know him,
> because he is with you, he is in you. (John 14:16-17)

According to the notes of the Jerusalem Bible: "The Greek word *parakletos* is here translated 'Advocate,' but it is difficult to choose between the possible meanings: 'advocate,' 'intercessor,' 'counselor,' 'protector,' 'support.' The parallel between the Spirit's work for the disciples and Christ's brings out powerfully the personal character of the Spirit." Furthermore, the very closeness of the Spirit to the disciples recalls the closeness of Wisdom and God's counsel to the prophets and counselors of the Old Testament.

The role of the Holy Spirit as counselor is described on a number of occasions in the New Testament. In the gospels of (Mark 13:11) and Luke (12:11-12), the disciples are advised not to worry when they are brought before the powers of this world to give witness, for it is the Holy Spirit that will teach them, even speak for them. Here the work of the prophets and counselors of the Old Testament is achieved in a new way. In the New Testament, Jesus promises that the Holy Spirit is there simply for the asking. (Luke 11:13) In the Book of Acts, the Holy Spirit descends on the disciples. Immediately, the disciples are able to speak God's message, his counsel. The power of the Spirit is so strong that they are able, to their amazement, to overcome the problem of the different languages of their listeners. Everyone who repents and is baptized in the name of Jesus Christ is told by Peter that they will receive the gift of the Holy Spirit. (Acts 2:38)

The power of the Holy Spirit continued to be active in the early church, and in particular took on the role of counselor in her major decisions, for example, the admission of pagans (Acts 8:29,40; 10:19,44-47; 11:12-16; 15:8); the decision not to place unnecessary burdens of the law on the pagan converts (Acts 15:28) and Paul's mission to the pagan world. (Acts 13:2; 16:6-7)

In 1 Corinthians (2:10-16), there is a significant passage which summarizes the new relationship of the church with the Holy Spirit:

> These are the very things that God has revealed to us through the Spirit, for the Spirit reaches the depths of everything, even the depths of God. After all, the depths of a man can only be known by his own spirit, not by any other man, and in the same way the depths of God can only be known by the Spirit of God. Now instead of the spirit of the world, we have received the Spirit that comes from God, to teach us to understand the gifts that he has given us. Therefore we teach, not in the way in which philosophy is taught, but in the way that the Spirit teaches us: we teach spiritual things spiritually. An unspiritual person is one who does not accept anything of the Spirit of God: he sees it all as nonsense; it is beyond his understanding because it can only be understood by means of the Spirit. A spiritual man, on the other hand, is able to judge the value of everything, and his own value is not to be judged by other men. As scripture says: Who can know the mind of the Lord, so who can teach him? But we are those who have the mind of Christ.

We have here the solution to the second paradox posed earlier by Proverbs:

> Counsel in another's heart is like deep water, but a discerning person will draw it up. (Prv 20:5) (REB)

It is impossible for the spirit of this world, trapped by sin and as such unable to love, to plumb the depths of another person. This is only possible for the person who has received the gift of the Spirit of God. Indeed, the gift is given so that the spiritual person can understand the workings of the

Spirit in the depths of the other. Paul stresses that this process is a gift: it cannot be fabricated by the spirit or the methods (philosophy) of this world alone.

Just as Jesus is present to us in the world yesterday and today, so the same Spirit that was present in the first century church is also present in the church of today. Yet, that the Spirit is present in counseling has, for the most part, been forgotten or very poorly understood. As a result, there has been a dangerous split between ecclesiology and counseling: on the one hand, counseling has been seen as primarily a secular activity with perhaps some spiritual elements tacked on; on the other hand, the church has been regarded as an institution that primarily looks after the spiritual well-being of the person, in isolation from the vital human concerns which counseling addresses. One of the reasons for the poor understanding of the connections between church and counseling has been the failure to acknowledge the self-revelation of God in the world outside the boundaries of the church.

GOD'S PROVIDENCE REVEALED IN THE WORLD

What then can we say about God's providence and human counseling in the late twentieth century? Firstly, of course, the cultural forms of counseling today are, in many ways, different from those in scriptural times. In the last one hundred years, there has been an explosion in knowledge and theory about the human condition and about the world in which we live. This knowledge has not only affected our thinking, but the very way in which we live out our material lives — the growth of technology is one obvious example. Yet, the need for counsel today is as great as it ever was — some might argue, greater than ever before. We have seen two world wars; hundreds of small wars; the advent of the nuclear bomb; the holocaust; and the threat of total environmental degradation. All these catastrophes (and more) have had a devastating effect on the social, psychological, emotional and spiritual lives of individuals and populations. The need for counsel, aimed firstly at avoiding such problems of our age and secondly at ameliorating the worst effects of such problems when they do occur, is urgent.

Christians believe that the counsel we need so urgently comes ultimately from God, because God's counsel is about God's loving relationship with people. God calls us to love God and to love one another. Counseling, as we now know it, is one response to that call. Yet I believe that counseling has a special place in the working out of God's providence, for it is primarily concerned with the freeing and enabling of others to love and to participate in the life that is God. Such counsel is resolutely opposed to the building of weapons of mass destruction, and the socially sanctioned degradation of both humans and their environment that has marked our age and which so limits the propensity to love.

Christian counseling is distinctive because it aims to open up the possibility of re-telling and re-creating the Christian story of love, whether those counseled are Christian or not. It is never the role of the Christian counselor to proselytize, which is a corruption of the counseling relationship, and a breach of trust. This is because proselytizing has come to mean valuing the process of conversion more highly than the individual to be converted and the subsequent devaluing of that person's unique experiences. Rather, it is the role of the counselor to listen closely and to sound the depths of an individual or family. It is the belief and experience of Christians that at the core of each person is a spirit capable of, indeed requiring, communion with the loving Spirit of God. This communion can take many forms, and it is not restricted to the forms endorsed by religious denominations in their present form. It is any counselor's aim to draw out the human spirit which, for whatever reason, has become restricted.

For many people today, the call to love others — let alone God — may appear to be emotionally, psychologically, culturally or structurally impossible. People often complain to counselors of dead and blunted feelings, of continuing bitter anger, of annoying behavioral problems that interfere with their relationships. In response, counselors can set in motion a two-fold process: at one level, the counselor can tap into the basically healthy, authentic part of the person which makes growth and love possible; while at another level the counselor works to remove impediments to love and growth. The first level is that which God gifted to the person and, in the words of Genesis, saw that "It was good." The second level represents the various restrictions within the society, the family, the individual or wherever, that hamper the person expressing that goodness. "I am sent to proclaim liberty to captives," says Jesus. This theme of liberty and freedom is one which I will come back to again and again, for it is the theme that informs much of the practical work of counseling. It is in this dual sense that the counseling process enables individuals to respond to God's call, in accordance with God's providential will for them.

Love and Freedom: Integral to Christian Counseling

LOVE: AS THEME OF COUNSELING

A first task for a counselor is to establish a relationship of love with the counselee which mirrors and participates in God's action as counselor. Thomas Hart speaks of the counselor in this role as "sacrament, the visible expression of the invisible."[1] It is possible to stimulate change without establishing this loving relationship, but in Christian terms such change will at best be accidental to God's purposes and at worst against God's providence. This is because, as argued earlier, underlying God's providence and at its core is the call to an ever deeper and more loving relationship.

The loving relationship of counseling is of a special kind. It is not the same as a marital or sexual relationship, nor a parent/child relationship, nor a relationship between friends. Yet it contains some of the dynamism of all these relationships and, within their connectedness, each party gives a great deal of themselves. On the counselee's part, there is the courage to lay bare a part of the self that is in need of change, transformation or healing. For the counselor, there is the effort to sustain authenticity of self as he/she works with the counselee to remove impediments to growth. Oliver Morgan describes this ongoing stance of the counselor in terms of "compassion, steadfast love and faithfulness."[2] Change occurs within the context of the close counseling relationship, and not only in the counselee, but also in the counselor. Counselors recognize impediments to growth in counselees for the very reason that they are the same as, or similar to, their own.

Impediments to growth are many, but common to all is the absence of love. It is not only an absence of love in, say, the family or in immediate relationships that troubles people, but also an absence in their culture, society and world. The loving relationship of counseling is important because, without it, the underlying cause of many other problems cannot adequately be addressed. The special kind of love in the counseling relationship strengthens and frees the counselee to mobilize other unrecognized strengths, both internal psycho-spiritual strengths and external family-societal-cultural strengths, which can then be brought to bear upon the problems that have seemed insurmountable.

FREEDOM: AS THEME OF COUNSELING

For us as Christians, love and freedom are intimately connected because a loving God sets us free, so that we can freely love. (Luke 4:18-21) "Love and do as you will," says St. Augustine. Many people who seek counseling are trapped in situations where love seems impossible. Commonly, they are living in families or relationships which, far from being the springboards for growth they should be and even may want to be, are closed systems of interlocking, mutually dysfunctional roles and belief structures — some so rigid as to be constricting, others so fluid as to be dangerously confusing. Liberation in all its forms is a major theme of counseling.

The liberation that occurs in counseling is the freeing of the person to love. At the heart of the need for personal counseling is the need for love. But then, too, the greatest need of society is love, and its greatest deficit is the absence of love. Such is the horror of our modern situation that we are forced to deny, sometimes most emphatically, that love is lacking, be it in society or in ourselves. We pretend that love is free and effortless, something we can get and give as easily as the air we breathe. We deny that our need for love is our deepest yearning and one that is not being fulfilled. Denying reality, we further isolate ourselves from the opportunity to love and be loved and shield ourselves with ideologies and myths that entrap us. Most dangerously, perhaps, we accept as good and right our love-deprived and unfree culture when there is neither rational nor Christian basis for such judgment. Over a period of forty years, Jacques Ellul has critiqued the way in which technology increasingly constricts human freedom, while sustaining the illusion of stimulating human capacity to act freely.[3]

> With the final integration of the instinctive and the spiritual by means of these human techniques, the edifice of the technical society will be completed. It will not be a universal concentration camp, for it will be guilty of no atrocity. It will not be insane, for everything will be ordered, and the stains of human passion will be lost amid the chromium gleam. We shall have nothing more to lose, and nothing to win. Our deepest instincts and our most secret passions will be analyzed, published and exploited. We shall be rewarded with everything our hearts ever desired. And the supreme luxury of the society of technical necessity will be to grant the bonus of useless revolt and of an acquiescent smile.[4]

There is an almost infinite variety of ways in which individuals and groups can become trapped in loveless and isolated circumstances which interfere with their ability to respond to the call of love. Thinking about this area, I have found the liberation theologian, Gustavo Gutiérrez, particularly helpful. Gutiérrez comments that:

> The truth that sets human beings free is Jesus himself... The task imposed on those whom he sets free (see Jn 8:36) and this includes Christian counselors is to proclaim the saving

truth that he came to bring us. The salvation in question I have been calling integral liberation, because, with liberation from sin as its starting point, it extends to all dimensions of the human.[5]

Gutiérrez identifies three levels of liberation which, though distinct and relatively autonomous, together make a unified concept of liberation. The three levels he identifies are: social liberation, the freedom of the human person and full communion. Gutiérrez's framework can assist us explore the meanings of freedom in the counseling situation.

At the first level, that of social liberation, Gutiérrez quotes with approval the Catholic church document *Libertatis Conscientia*:

Awareness of human freedom and dignity, together with the affirmation of the inalienable rights of individuals and peoples, is one of the major characteristics of our time. But freedom demands conditions of an economic, social, political and cultural kind, which make possible its full exercise. A clearer perception of the obstacles that hinder its development and offend human dignity is at the source of the powerful aspirations to liberation at work in our world. (no 1; see nos.17 and 61).[6]

I believe Gutiérrez is right: individual and family problems are rarely self-contained, but compounded or created by unjust societal structures. Many families receive inadequate wages for their work, or need to pay out large amounts of money in usurious interest rates, or have unemployed members because of a policy of high unemployment. These families are experiencing not only personal distress, but also social injustice. Injustices, and our acquiescence in them, create practical problems such as poverty and also produce a legacy of resentment that inhibits the growth of love within the individual or family. We are accustomed to think of counselors as primarily concerned with individuals or families. However, this is far from true. Many experienced counselors are keen to apply their insights to the wider society and particularly to public policy,[7] because good counselors, like their predecessors in the Old Testament, tend to look both to the individual and to the wider context of the individual's life.

The second level, the freedom of the human person, Gutiérrez sees as a deeper level of liberation in which:

> Humankind is seen as assuming conscious responsibility for its own destiny. Social structures always depend on human persons and real change must involve them. This understanding provides a dynamic context and broadens the horizon of the desired social changes. In this perspective the unfolding of all the dimensions of humanness is demanded—persons who make themselves throughout their life and throughout history.[8]

Gutiérrez makes a further distinction: "A change of social structures can help to bring about this personal change but does not automatically bring it about." Similarly, changes in individuals do not necessarily bring about societal change,[9] an important distinction because most current counseling operates at the level of individual change.

Finally, Gutiérrez believes that the saving work of Christ is primarily a deliverance from sin, which is the most radical form of slavery, the most radical evil and the source of other slaveries and other evils. It is the grace of Christ that liberates us from sin and enables us to live in communion. Because sin is radical evil, it can be conquered only by the grace of God and the radical liberation that the Lord bestows. This grace of God is present in every act of authentic love, which is why love is central in Christian counseling — without it, we cannot hope to affect the core of the counselee's problem(s). The opposition between grace and sin is played out in the inmost depths of every human person.

Liberation from sin is one side of the coin; the other is communion with God and others where "freedom from" becomes "freedom for." By nailing sin to the cross, Jesus opened the way for us to find full communion with the Father, a communion which discloses the meaning of our lives. The entire process of liberation is directed toward communion.[10]

One of the strengths of counseling is that it often makes explicit links between the various levels Gutiérrez describes. For instance, the type of paid employment which family members undertake (the social level), directly affects both the individuals involved and the family as a whole (the human person level): there are issues of pay; of job satisfaction; of hours worked; of identity in so far as it is associated with occupation; of social status and of general levels of stress. Each of these factors positively or negatively affects the way the individual or family function as well as the way they make sense of their life and construct a sense of meaning (the communion level).

Identifying the sources of problems helps the counselor determine the sort of counseling that is necessary and appropriate. To set out to psychoanalyze a person whose problems arise primarily from a current experience of racism would not only be inappropriate but insulting. Counseling might, however, assist that person to deal directly with racists or with racist attitudes or structures that constrain the person's freedom to love and be loved.

UNCONDITIONAL LOVE: THE COUNSELING IDEAL

In the Christian view, what is central to and underlies our problems is a disruption of a person's loving relationship with God, and central to this disruption is our refusal to act as though a loving God made us, and our refusal to accept the corollary that we thereby have intrinsic worth. For the Christian, love flows from the unconditional love of the Trinity, of which Creation is an expression, and all relationships are, ideally, relationships of unconditional love. Efforts to establish relationships on any other basis eventually lead to love becoming a conditional concept.

Suffering and injury are the consequences of conditional love. Children who are loved only if they are well-behaved, or bright, or pretty, suffer deeply in their sense of self-esteem: in many families it is common for the child who is loved conditionally to become the child who is not loved at all. Workers who are valued only for the work they do, that is, conditionally, eventually become but cogs in the machine. Racism and war originate in a conditional love of only those who are similar which escalates to destroy love and life.

It is not easy to love unconditionally, and we all fail constantly. If love is to be unconditional, then there has to be forgiveness. In the counseling situation, it is common to meet people whose major problem is their failure to forgive themselves or others. But the forgiveness they and we need is not something always within our capacity to control. We cannot force ourselves to forgive. Yet without forgiveness, our lives are narrowed and demeaned. As the Christian sees it, forgiveness is a gift from God, because through Christ "we gain our freedom, the forgiveness of our sins." (Eph 1:7) Wherever forgiveness is present, there is the powerful action of God.

Often people are unaware of the need for forgiveness. They may feel a righteous anger against those who have hurt them, especially parents. The failure to forgive, or even to see the need to forgive, results in a rigidity in relationships with a concomitant fragile moral uprightness that seems constantly in danger of collapse, because, allied with lack of forgiveness, is a deep sense of guilt. If my parent or the person who has hurt me cannot be forgiven, then logically neither can I. In my unforgiving universe, I must fly into the denial of reality or make superhuman efforts to be perfect. Both alternatives seriously limit the possibilities for loving relationships. In the pain and suffering we experience, it is little wonder that the forgiveness of sins is such a joyous event and so central to the Christian message.

Forgiveness restores the healthy interrelatedness between people that expresses most fully who we and they are. Forgiveness frees us from past memories and experiences of injustice and hurt. These memories may be individual memories and experiences, such as crippling memories of child abuse, or they may be corporate and cultural memories, such as the international memory of events like Auschwitz which become a universal hurt. In every country there are needs for forgiveness and a reconciliation with the past, so that people can lay to rest memories that persist over generations. Unresolved memories of past injustices disrupt the unconscious life of both individuals and societies, and eventually disrupt people's relationships in the here and now.

THE NEED FOR JUSTICE AND MERCY

While forgiveness and reconciliation can heal the pain and promote the growth of love, they are incomplete without justice and mercy. Indigenous people may forgive whites for the injustices of the past but, if these injustices continue, there can be no real freedom, no forgiveness and no loving relationships. Families, too, can be unjust and merciless. Rather than havens of positive, caring, nurturing love, they can become places in which the members are constantly exploited by those more powerful: young children by parents, wives by husbands, aged parents by adult children. From a very young age, children feel injustice deeply, particularly when they perceive their parents or powerful others whom they love to be unjust.

The Christian concern for justice is beautifully expressed in the letter to the Ephesians (6:4): "And parents, never drive your children to resentment but in bringing them up correct them and guide them as the Lord does." The instruction does not imply a *laissez-faire* attitude to child-rearing. Rather, it demands that parents act as God does, with justice. It is not a justice obsessed with the letter of the law, but one concerned with the higher levels of perspective taking and fairness described by Kohlberg, in which the perspective of each of the family members is fairly considered,[11] as well as the concern for responsibility and maintaining a caring relationship as described by Gilligan.[12] Correction without justice breeds resentment, or "wrath," as the King James version translates the term in Ephesians. There is so much possible abuse of power in parenting: correcting children to suit the wants of the parent rather than the needs of the child, favoring one child over another or passing to children responsibilities that are rightly those of the parents. Of course, all parents fail in their attempts to be "good parents," as do children in their often tremendous strivings to please their parents. Both need each other's mercy and forgiveness and love. A family without mercy is a very cold place in which to grow up, and a parent who is without mercy cannot be said to be guiding "as the Lord does." While mercy is the celebration of love, a family that is all mercy without justice cannot sustain love, for justice is the backbone that love needs in order to grow. Many attempts to solve the problem of juvenile delinquency fail because we are unable to reconcile the two concepts and, instead, totter recklessly from one to the other. The resolution of issues of justice and mercy are central to Christian counseling, not only in the family, but also in the wider community.

THE EXPERIENCE OF MEANINGLESSNESS

Many people who seek counseling are experiencing a profound sense of meaninglessness in their lives. They cling to distractions — drugs, alcohol, some forms of madness, the never-ending accumulation of goods and power. Where meaning is absent, love makes no sense. The absence of meaning can be a particularly powerful form of entrapment: life without meaning is horrifying, but the distractions the person chases to avoid the experience of meaninglessness often become addictive and problems in their own right.

Jesus described himself as the Way, the Truth and the Life. (Jn 14:6) In Christian counseling, if meaning is to re-emerge through counseling, people need to be brought back in touch with this Jesus whose very existence gives meaning to reality. This is not just a matter of cognitive knowledge, of telling or reminding people about Jesus. It is primarily the experience of the counselor "being" Jesus. Oliver Morgan, in what he describes as a "healing christology," comments: "The pastoral counselor becomes for the client a personalized point of meeting with God's gracious activity, and discovers (often surprisingly) herself or himself becoming God's presence."[13] This is especially true when the issue of death, which is a challenge to all meaning systems, arises.

THE QUESTION OF DEATH

If death cannot be integrated into the meaning system of a person, neither can life. Every death presents a meaning problem. Some deaths present particularly daunting problems, especially the deaths of children, painful deaths, suicides, deaths of those with parental responsibilities, plane or motor vehicle caused deaths, murders, deaths in war, and more lately deaths from cancer and AIDS. While there are counseling techniques available to help survivors cope with the distress that they experience and to help those preparing to die — even to help prevent unjust or avoidable deaths — death by its finality challenges the very structure of every individual's life. Though Christians may believe in an afterlife, death brings to an end that which is most familiar and precious now, and (for Christians) death has not lost its forsakenness. Jesus himself cries out, "My God, my God! Why have you forsaken me?" (Mt 27:46) (REB) There are no easy answers, no easy consolations. To help, the counselor must enter the forsakenness of the dying and the bereaved, in the way of Jesus of the Incarnation and the Crucifixion.[14] Only through entering into the death experienced by the counselee does the power and the freedom of the resurrection become possible in the counseling relationship.

TO SEE MORE CLEARLY

It is so easy to deceive ourselves and to collude in collective self-deception when we face the problems of lovelessness, entrapment, injustice, suffering, meaninglessness and death. Deceit, itself, is a major form of entrapment, and is endemic in the political, business, media and military arenas of our society, amongst others. Set against this, Christians believe that God is Truth. In the Gospel of John, Jesus calls the devil "a liar, and the father of lies." (John 8:44) A great strength of good counseling is that it can cut through many kinds and degrees of deceit. The person, the family, the society that is counseled has to attend to realities previously obscured. The act of seeing more clearly is in itself liberating, (and the blind see), and acting on insight even more so. Through action, the counselee maintains the insight and does not fall back into self-deception and illusion. The dynamic process of counseling stimulates insight, followed by action, which in turns leads to further insight, and then yet further action, and so on. Hence, liberation is both stimulated and maintained.

In this chapter I have sought to show how counseling can and should be part of God's providential action. Counseling is far more than a collection of therapeutic techniques but shares in God's liberating and loving participation in the world. We, as Christian counselors, need to be open to this dimension of our work if we are to appreciate properly the significance of the work that we have undertaken.

---

[1] Hart, Thomas, "Counseling's Spiritual Dimension: Nine Guiding Principles," *The Journal of Pastoral Care, 1989, Vol.43, No.2, p.117.*
[2] Morgan, Oliver J., "Elements in a Spirituality of Pastoral Care," *The Journal of Pastoral Care*, 1989, Vol.43, No.2, p.102.
[3] Ellul, Jacques, *The Technological Society*, Vintage Books, New York, 1964; through to Ellul, Jacques, *The Technological Bluff*, Wm. B. Eerdman Publishing Co., Grand Rapids, 1990.
[4] Ellul, Jacques, *The Technological Society*, Vintage Books, New York, 1964, pp.426-427.
[5] Gutiérrez, G., *The Truth Shall Make You Free*, Orbis Books, Maryknoll, New York, 1990, p.141.
[6] ibid, p.129.
[7] See, for instance, Goldstein, Joseph; Freud, Anna; Solnit, Albert J., *Beyond the Best Interests of the Child*, The Free Press, Macmillan Publishing Co., New York, 1973. Winnicott, Donald W., *Deprivation and Delinquency*, Tavistock Publications, London, 1984. Minuchin, Salvador, *Family Kaleidoscope*, Harvard University Press, Cambridge, 1984.
[8] Gutiérrez, op.cit., pp.132-133.
[9] ibid, p.133.
[10] ibid, pp.135-141.
[11] Kohlberg, L., *The Philosophy of Moral Development*, Harper and Row, San Francisco, 1981.
[12] Gilligan, C., *In a Different Voice; Psychological Theory and Women's Development*, Harvard University Press, Cambridge, Mass., 1982.
[13] Morgan, op.cit., p.106.
[14] For a sensitive account of this issue see Hauerwas, Stanley, *Naming the Silences: God, Medicine, and the Problem of Suffering*, Wm. B. Eerdman Publishing Co., Grand Rapids, 1990.

4

Growing in Faith and Love

IMAGES OF GOD

Each of us has different images of God. The images that counselors have of God affect their style of counseling, because the way we name God affects the way we act for God. Moses was aware of this when he said to God in the burning bush: "I am to go then to the sons of Israel and say to them, 'The God of our fathers has sent me to you.' But if they ask me what his name is, what am I to tell them?" God replies, "I Am who I Am. This," he added, "is what you must say to the sons of Israel: 'I Am has sent me to you.'" (Ex 3:13-15) God's reply to Moses goes beyond any of our images of God. All images falter when faced with the "I AM" of God, even the word "God" itself.

Gregory Baum, amongst others, has made the point that:
> God is always and exclusively subject. . . People are, in part, objects; God is in no way object. God is always and irreducibly subject. There is nothing we can know about him or say about him unless he reveals himself, unless he chooses to speak. . .what is required for the knowledge of God is a special openness to his voice called faith.[1]

God then is a God who comes to us and who cannot be discovered by our own efforts unaided. While our images of God come first from God, as part of God's self-revelation, this does not alter the fact that images of God, as all other images, are also projections of our own human experience. We can only understand from a human perspective. But projection is not necessarily bad or wrong, and God uses our projections to disclose aspects of God.

Our images of God come from a variety of sources. The best known and most used source of images in the Christian tradition is scripture. In the scriptures we find a multitude of images of God, including the image of God as counselor which we explored in Chapter Two. There are also images of God as King, as Judge, as Lord, as Lover, as Messiah, as Savior, as Liberator, as Friend, as Father and even as Mother. The very diversity of images of God alerts us that no one image, however attractive, is sufficient.

Images of God are not neutral cognitive events, but a call from God to action in the here and now. God gives us images appropriate to our part in the working out of God's providence. Baum comments that, "Every sentence about God can be translated into a declaration about human life,"[2] and Fowler has made the point that all metaphors used to represent God in the scriptures are relational.[3] For my part, I believe that we cannot truly understand, or even perceive, these images unless we enter into the relationship which they signify. That is, we cannot understand God as king unless we become the loyal servant; God as lover unless we become the beloved; God as liberator unless we become the liberated; God as friend unless we become friends of God. Not only do such images call us into relationship with God, but they simultaneously call us into relationship with the world. Thus, when we see God as the suffering servant, we are both served by that servant and also serve others in their suffering. Just as the servant of the King is about the King's business, the lover shares that love with the world, the child of God sees all as brothers and sisters, and so on.

IMAGES AND WORLD VIEW

Christians have constantly generated new images. They range from the popular sixteenth century devotion to the "sacred heart" in some Catholic circles to the Christian existentialists' imagining of God as the "eschatological ground of being."

Because all the various images of God are, in part, projections of the human condition, each image reflects a deeper understanding of how people conceive the world — what Sallie McFague calls the root-metaphor.[4] For many, images of God now have to incorporate evolution, relativity, the unconscious and technology because we live in an age in which our understanding of the world and how humans interact with it has greatly changed. If God is absent from any area, then God is not God. Institutional churches have not always been able to generate images that fit the modern person's experience of the call of God. For example, the image of the good shepherd loses some of its power when addressed to Christians living in a metropolis. Though in recent years there has been a great deal of work done to generate more appropriate images for the Australian church,[5] much necessary work remains.

Then, too, though we live in and share one world, there are a variety of ways we can conceive of that world — perhaps as a huge interacting organism or, mechanistically, as long chains of causes and effects or even as a flat disc floating in space. It is, in fact, common for the modern person to have a number of world views or images. For most of us, our vision of the world is only partly conscious, formed as it is by our family, our culture, our education and the variety of life events that shape us. What is certain is that few of us now share the world view described in the book of Genesis: a flat world floating on a sea of water, and protected from the waters above by the great dome of the sky.

For Christian counselors, it is important whether the images we have of the world complement or collide with our images of God. This raises a number of questions: if the images are complementary, is this good or bad? It may be problematic if a comfortable middle-class Christian constantly projects images of a comfortable middle-class God, for in such a world view, complemented by the image of God, there is no need for liberation and hence it is difficult to appreciate the image of God as liberator which is so integral to Christian counseling. If the images are not complementary, what are we to make of this? For example, Christian fundamentalism can place an intolerable intellectual burden on people by insisting that their world view meshes with an image of a God who created the world in seven days.

Ultimately, as we have seen earlier, all images of God are insufficient. Similarly, because it seems unlikely that humans will ever be able to imagine the world in all its complexity, it is wise to be highly sceptical of any image of God that meshes perfectly with an image of the world. At the same time, when images of God and the world do not at least have common boundaries, this indicates that the images of one or both are unrealistic or inadequate. There can be no call from a God who is completely outside the world. Finally, where images of God and images of the world collide, there is the challenge to address seriously the shortcomings of one or other or both images.

There are, however, other images of God that are projections of evil, which occurs "when the human heart freely turns from its proper good and becomes perverted in its goals,"[6] and these do not reflect God, and nothing of God is revealed in them. I think here, for instance, of the images of God that justify apartheid. There are also images of God that help to legitimate unjust class divisions: the image of God as omnipotent might console the comfortable middle-class, but threaten and oppress those suffering as a result of long-standing and apparently intractable social injustice. In this case the poor ask, "Why doesn't the omnipotent God help?"[7] Similarly, feminism has alerted us to the fact that patriarchal images of God can bind women and disinherit them from the good news of God's self-revelation. Furthermore, the use of patriarchal images has tended to squeeze out and diminish legitimate ways of talking about God in a female voice. Elizabeth Johnson has shown how the female image of God as Wisdom, *Sophia* in the Greek, has been systematically downplayed or ignored. As a result, basically healthy images of God such as Spirit and Trinity have been undermined and become symbols of the subordination of women.[8] Patriarchal, and indeed all images of God can be subverted into vehicles of oppression when it is forgotten that God is always more unlike, than like, any image we can perceive. There is a great wisdom in the Buddhist maxim, "If you see the Buddha, kill him."

IMAGES AND FAITH: FOWLER'S STAGES OF FAITH DEVELOPMENT

Another factor that affects the counselor's image of God is the counselor's faith development. In understanding this area, James Fowler's work on the stages of faith is most helpful.[9] Fowler has drawn on the insights of Piaget, Erikson, Kohlberg and other developmental psychologists, as well as his own detailed work, to argue that faith is a universal human characteristic with a developmental dynamic, not unlike the dynamics of cognitive, psychological and moral development. Fowler identifies seven stages of faith, each of which has an optimum chronological age range, and he believes that the ways we use and construct symbols in our efforts to create meaning are markedly different in each stage. It follows that our images of God are also different in each stage. The stages and the optimum ages at which they may develop are: primal faith during infancy; intuitive-projective faith from age 3–7; mythic-literal faith from age 7–12; synthetic-conventional faith from age 12–18; individuative-reflective faith from age 18–35; conjunctive faith from age 35 on and finally universalizing faith which is extremely rare.

When we think of the images that a preschool child might have of God, it is relatively easy to see that these will generally be different from the images that a middle-aged person will have, and that these differences are not just explained by differing levels of experience or education, but also by the differing levels of cognitive, psycho-social and moral development of the two persons. As a person grows and matures, so too does the way they imagine God. At each developmental stage there are differing types of image appropriate for that age. It would be foolish, for instance, to expect a four year old child to have a similar image of God to that of a forty-four year old. While differences are usually quite evident when we are comparing adults' and children's images of God it is more difficult to compare images that adults have at different levels of development. To further complicate the picture, it is apparent to even the most casual observer that there are some adults whose faith has not changed substantially since childhood. Such a childlike faith can be problematic when the adult has to face the challenges of adulthood.

While Fowler's first four stages of faith develop, optimally, during childhood and adolescence, many adults never move beyond a child's or adolescent's stage of faith. Indeed, Fowler comments that the developmental level at which adults tend to settle in most middle-class American churches is best described in terms of synthetic-conventional faith (that is, of an age appropriate for 12–18 year olds), or just beyond it.[10] It is therefore important not to ignore images which, though having their origin in a stage of faith more appropriate for children, still powerfully influence the ways many adults shape their faith experience.

Let's look at Fowler's stages so that we can better appreciate the differences in developmentally generated images of God experienced by both counselees and counselors.

Primal Faith: In primal faith, the seeds of trust, courage, hope and love are sown and must contend with sensed threats of abandonment, inconsistencies and deprivations in an infant's environment. Mutuality, trust, autonomy, hope and courage, or their opposites, develop in this phase, and underlie or threaten to undermine, all that comes later in faith development. It is, of course, rare for adults' faith development to be arrested at this level and it usually occurs only where there are substantial delays in intellectual development. At this stage, the small child is aware of the presence of God, mediated through the caring presence of others.

Intuitive-Projective Stage: This stage is the birth of the imagination, and images of God are relatively fluid. Childhood fantasies are unrestrained by logical thought, and the imagination is extremely productive of long-lasting images and feelings, positive and negative, that will later have to be ordered and sorted so that the adult can attain a more consistent meaning in life. Again, it is relatively rare for adults to get stuck at this stage, though this may occur sometimes when there is intellectual impairment, or in some forms of mental illness.

Mythic-Literal Stage: Moving to this level, the person begins to take on for him/herself the stories, beliefs and observances that symbolize his or her belonging to a community. Beliefs are appropriated with literal interpretations, as are moral rules and attitudes. Symbols are understood as one-dimensional and literal in meaning. This is the stage when the narrative in story, drama and myth is an important way to find and give coherence to experience. Some adult Christians, it seems, stay at this stage indefinitely. Characteristically, they tend to interpret images literally, and their desire to mold their lives to fit preconceived images can lead to a stilted perfectionism, or a demeaning sense of "badness" because of mistreatment, neglect or the apparent disfavor of significant others. Adults who remain at this stage will often hold tenaciously to safe images from their childhood. Great love, patience and understanding is needed to help such people, for to do so will mean their leaving behind images that have helped them survive in a hostile, sad or frightening childhood environment.

Synthetic-Conventional Stage: The person at this stage, and at about 12–18 years, tends to see their world in interpersonal terms. It is a "conformist" stage in the sense that the person is acutely tuned to the expectations and judgements of significant others and, as yet, does not have a sure enough grasp on his or her own identity and autonomous judgement to construct and maintain an independent perspective. While beliefs and values are deeply felt, they are usually tacitly held. The person has not yet stepped outside them to examine them explicitly or systematically.

In this synthetic-conventional stage, the person is able to form their own personal myth, linking their past and hoped for future, into an image of their ultimate world held together by characteristics of their personality. The personal myth can be thought of as the person's dream about themselves that gives their life coherence. The poets Donni and George Betts sum up some of the feelings of this stage when they write:

> A person's dream
> is not important
> because it does
> or does not happen,
> but because
>   it could happen.[11]

During this stage of faith development, it is important that the Christian integrates images of God into the growing personal myth that is being created. Otherwise, God becomes increasingly irrelevant to the person as they develop, a commonly witnessed event during adolescence.

There is also another hazard: that the images become so internalized that the person loses the ability to separate the image from the self and later loses the ability to judge and act independently of these images, or despairs when it becomes apparent that the images are inadequate. In other words, images and fantasy life can become so attractive, and people identify with them so fully, that there is great trauma when people have to face the often harsh realities of young adulthood or late adolescence. However, if the stage is negotiated successfully, there is a sense that this growth in personal myth is leading forward. George Betts describes well this transition to the individuative-reflective stage:

> My mind is wandering again,
>   going its own directions.
> I'm not afraid
>   just to let it be . . .
> It will flow
>   and take me
>   to new places,
>   exciting ideas,
> and feelings
>   beyond my present understanding.
> I will be richer . . .
> My journey will build
>   a bridge for my tomorrow.[12]

The Individuative-Reflective Stage: The self now claims an identity no longer defined by the composite of one's roles or meanings to others. To sustain the new identity, the self composes a meaning frame, conscious of its own boundaries and inner connections and aware of its own world view. Self (identity) and outlook (world view) are differentiated from those of others, and become acknowledged factors in the reactions, interpretations and judgements one makes of the actions of the self and others. This stage typically translates symbols into conceptual meanings. It is a "demythologising" stage. Images of God, self and world which were previously uncritically accepted are taken apart and examined piece by piece. The hazard of this stage is an excessive confidence in the conscious mind and in critical thought, as well as a kind of narcissism in which the now clearly bounded and reflective self overassimilates "reality" and the perspectives of others into its own world view. I am reminded of the various "isms" to which people in our society can become addicted.

Conjunctive Faith: This penultimate stage entails the integration (of self and worldview), of much that was suppressed or unrecognized in the interest of the previous stage's self-certainty and conscious adaptation to reality. People now develop a "second naivete" in which they reunite symbolic power with conceptual meanings. Here there must be a new reclaiming and reworking of one's past. There must be an opening to the voices of one's deeper self. Importantly, this stage involves a critical recognition of one's social unconscious — the myths, ideal images and prejudices built deeply into the self system by virtue of one's nurture within a particular social class, religious tradition, ethnic group or the like. Unusual before midlife, conjunctive faith knows the sacrament of defeat and the reality of irrevocable commitments and actions.

Whereas the hallmark of the previous stage was the struggle to clarify boundaries of self and outlook, the characteristic of this stage is the attempt to make these realities porous and permeable. Alive to paradox and truth in apparent contradictions, the person strives to unify opposites in mind and experience. The person at this stage generates and maintains vulnerability to the strange truths of those who are "other." Ironic imagination is now a great strength — the capacity to see and to participate in one's, or one's group's, most powerful meanings, while simultaneously recognizing that they are relative and inevitably distorting apprehensions of transcendent reality. The hazard of this stage is the paradoxical understanding of truth that can lead to a debilitating passivity and inaction, complacency or cynical withdrawal.

Universalizing Faith: The transition to the final stage of faith development requires an active overcoming of the paradoxes of conjunctive faith. Heedless of the threats to self, to primary groups and to the institutional arrangements of the present order, universalizing faith becomes a disciplined, activist incarnation (a making real and tangible) of the imperatives of absolute love and justice, of which conjunctive faith has partial apprehensions. The self, at this last stage, expends itself in the transformation of present reality in the direction of a transcendent reality that overcomes the shortcomings and the failures of present existence. Persons who have attained universalizing faith typically exhibit qualities that challenge our usual criteria of "normality." They are heedless of self-preservation, and the vividness of their task and their feel for a transcendent moral and religious reality give their actions and words an extraordinary and often unpredictable quality. As they penetrate our obsession with survival, security and significance, they threaten our measured standards of righteousness and goodness and prudence. Their leadership initiatives, which often involve strategies of nonviolent suffering and profound respect for life, constitute affronts to our usual notions of relevance. Images of God at this stage of faith are difficult to describe. They appear both new and old, but with a vitality that can blur the distinction between image and action, between the image and what it represents, between the image seen and the image seeing, between self and image, between self and God.

Fowler's work helps us to see that the images we have of God are developmental, that is, they are with us throughout our life and not just during our childhood. If Fowler's theories are correct, or if they at least point in a helpful direction, then we would expect, in a general sense, that counselors below the age of thirty-five would have images of God that reflected either an individuative-reflective stage of faith, or a synthetic-conventional stage or, rarely perhaps, a mythic-literal stage. Counseling would be virtually impossible for a person at an earlier faith stage. Over the age of thirty-five, we would expect increasing numbers of counselors to have images of God reflecting a conjunctive level of faith, though there would still be counselors whose images reflected earlier faith stages. Very occasionally, there would be counselors with an image of God that reflected a universalizing faith.

FAITH, IMAGES AND PATHS TO LOVE

The content of our faith, taught by the religious tradition to which we belong, is another factor that affects our images of God. Content includes doctrines, dogmas, rituals and teachings, as well as images of the world and of God. Images of God can play an important role in reinforcing the doctrines, dogmas and teachings. No denomination has a monopoly on the one true image of God. Each denomination has an orientation which highlights particular aspects of God but which, at the same time, does not capture God's fullness. As people grow in faith, they see that the images of their original faith community are provisional. However, it is rare that we lose them entirely: "once a Catholic, always a Catholic," and similar phrases attest to this common feature of faith development. The truths or images of God that we receive as young Christians are the foundation on which we later build.

IMAGES AND COUNSELING

We have seen so far that a counselor's image of God is affected by the world and culture in which the counselor lives and also by the counselor's faith development. We have mentioned, in passing, that the God image is also dependent on the part the counselor is playing in the working out of God's providence. For a counselor, this providence is partially reflected in the type of counseling the counselor is engaged in and the counselee or group of counselees to whom the counselor is called. The counselor needs to be able to call upon images of God appropriate to each type of counseling and each counselee or group of counselees, if he or she is to make sense of what he or she is doing at the level of faith. As we have seen in the previous chapter, Christians believe that the counsel we need so urgently comes ultimately from God, because God's counsel is about God's loving relationship with people, about God's providence. In every situation there is a loving, Divine providential will. Similarly, there are, in each situation, images of God, available to the counselor, consistent with that will.

These images are freely given by God and the counselor is free to take them or reject them. We may reject them because new images of God are both a call and a challenge. They challenge previously held images of God, the counselor's self-image and complacent images of the world. Hence, counselors might hold onto the image of God as rock and savior (a true enough image in itself) when the image of God as, say, suffering servant might be more appropriate and useful to both counselor and counselee. In this example, the resistance to change of image may be resistance to acknowledging the real suffering in the world in which Christ partakes. Similarly, a counselor who clings to the image of God as suffering servant may have trouble with the image we find in scripture of Christ removing the sellers from the temple. Perhaps this image challenges the counselor's self-denial of aggression. While a counselor does not have to accept an image, God's self-revelation is always a gift and is never coercion, and limiting our images of God may result in limiting our ability to counsel. The Christian counselor, to be effective, needs to pay attention to these images of God, which are not only God's self-revelation but also God's call. Unless we are aware of the images available to us, it is difficult to know whether we are doing God's will or acting in accordance with God's providence. With an awareness of God images, the counselor's self-examination needs to go on to test them against a number of criteria. Does this image fit with the world as we know it? If not, then perhaps the image is too "other worldly" and has not much to do with our practice. Does that image fit too closely with our world image? In this case, the image of God might more accurately be described as our image, and hence of little use in revealing God's will. Has the image of God remained static over many years? Perhaps this means we have stopped growing, opted for safety, and are no longer open to the newness of God's self-revelation. Does the image of God challenge us to a deeper and more loving relationship with God, the counselee and ourselves? This final question is crucial: without love and working within a world that is desperately in need of counsel, the Christian counselor has ultimately nothing to offer.

---

[1] Baum, Gregory, *Man Becoming: God in Secular Language,* Herder and Herder, New York, N.Y., 1970. pp.174-176.
[2] ibid., p.181.
[3] Fowler, James, *Faith Development and Pastoral Care,* Fortress Press, Philadelphia, 1987, pp.37-38.

[4] McFague, Sallie, *Models of God: Theology for an Ecological, Nuclear Age,* Fortress Press, Philadelphia, 1987.
[5] See for instance, Hannaford, John, *Under a Southern Cross,* The House Of Tabor, Unley Park, 1985. Kelly, Tony, *A New Imagining: Towards an Australian Spirituality,* Collins Dove, Melbourne, 1990. Stockton, Eugene D., *Land Marks: A Spiritual Search in a Southern Land,* Parish Ministry Publications, Eastwood, 1990. Thornhill, John, *Making Australia: Exploring our National Conversation,* Millennium Books, Newtown, 1992.
[6] Ormerod, Neil, *Grace & Disgrace: A Theology of Self-Esteem, Society and History,* E.J. Dwyer, Sydney, 1992, p.3.
[7] For a succinct criticism of the idea of God as omnipotent see Birch, Charles, *On Purpose: A New Thinking for the New Millenium,* New South Wales University Press, 1990, pp.93-94.
[8] Johnson, Elizabeth A., *She Who Is: The Mystery of God in Feminist Theological Discourse,* Crossroad, New York, 1992.
[9] Fowler, James, *Stages of Faith: The Psychology of Human Development and the Quest for Meaning,* Collins Dove, 1981.
[10] ibid. Blackburn, p.294.
[11] Betts, Donni and George, *Growing Together,* Celestial Arts, Millbrae, 1973.
[12] Betts, George, *Tears and Pebbles in my Pockets,* Celestial Arts, Millbrae, 1976.

Analysis and Conversion

FAITH AND SOCIAL REALITIES

Between the Christian counselor and the world there is always creative tension. While the tension is not rejection of the world nor retreat from it, neither is it wholesale acceptance. In scriptural terms, the Christian is "in" the world but not "of it." (John 17) This is a difficult position to maintain and few are able to achieve it for long. The world is good as a creation of God: at the same time the world is a damaged place in which there is great hurt and injustice. Both the good and the bad coexist within the one world and the Christian must struggle to maintain a perspective that acknowledges both these realities, the God-given and the disastrously flawed.

Christians have rarely, if ever, lived in a truly Christian society. Our society is driven by a number of forces, of which Christianity is only one, and many forces are antagonistic to the good news that Christ brings. It is arguable, for instance, that much modern economics is an attempt to obscure and justify greed. Greed is repulsive to the Christian message, yet greed and self-interest are widely accepted as the base of a democratic free enterprise economy such as our own. To what extent society is or has been affected by the Christian belief and action system varies from place to place, from time to time and from issue to issue. To a significant degree, the Christian belief system now appears to make few inroads into the dominant ideology of self-interest. The idea that the Christian God of love is of practical significance in the day to day social realities is an alien thought to the majority of people.

One of the advantages of having a Christian faith is our ability to take a step back from society and the world so that we may see them more clearly, for what they are, both in their glories and in their tragedies. Our perceived self-worth as Christians comes from God and not from the world or society and, though loving the world, we as Christians ultimately do not depend on it as a source of ultimate worth. Such a dependence on the world by Christians is rigorously attacked in scripture: "I am a jealous God." (Eccl) In this "stepping back," Christians also have a number of specific aids for analysis. Firstly, there is scripture itself, which cuts through the facades, the fantasies and the injustices of society and offers hope of striving for a new worthwhile order. As well, there is the Christian tradition, which can be a source of wisdom and inspiration in analyzing the world. Then, thirdly, there is the Christian community itself which, in its fellowship and in its sacramental life, can also be a source of support. Finally, there is prayer.

Prayer is our connection with God, the transcendent subject, who constantly confounds our smugness and our complacency about society. Prayer, though not analysis itself, is the foundation of Christian analysis. All analysis has a starting place, and there is no such thing as value free, objective analysis or research, although such a belief is one of the dominant myths of our age. Prayer gives us as Christians an orientation, and hence guides our analysis.

CHRISTIAN SOCIAL ANALYSIS

For Christians, analysis is not an objective activity devoid of feelings and values. Rather, its starting point is our subjective relationship with God, and our passionate ongoing commitment to this relationship. In an earlier chapter we have discussed God's providence. No valid Christian critique or analysis can be achieved outside of God's providence, and valid critique is part of that providence. Every Christian who is able to respond to the God of love is able to critique the world in which we live.

This is so because the Christian, once having entered the relationship of love, becomes sensitized to the fact that at times the world does not reflect this loving relationship. This is so even of very young Christians, who know of the love of God primarily through their families. Hence my three year old, when she senses that I am in a bad mood and not giving her the consistent loving attention that she has come to expect as normal, can tell me, "Daddy, stop being cross!" Often, the simplest critiques are both the best and the most accurate. It falls to only a few, with great intellectual gifts, integrity, courage and determination, to develop a wide ranging and complex criticism of the world and society. Such people are vitally necessary, but are not necessarily the role models for all Christians or counselors. What the ordinary Christian counselor needs is a critique consistent with God's call to him or her — a critique that enables him or her to respond appropriately to the needs of the counselee who requires assistance.

We will now turn more directly to the issues that need to be a part of a counselor's critique of the world. For a Christian, the act of analysis arises from the disjunction between the Kingdom of God, experienced as God's love for us and all creation in our ongoing conversion, and our experience of a sometimes brutal, hard, unloving world. By "world," I mean not just the external material world, but also the internal psychic world. We experience the disjunction of the Kingdom and the world as a tension that needs both understanding and action. The tension tells us that the Kingdom is at the same time here, and has not yet arrived. We are called to understand and act upon that little bit of "unKingdom" that stands before us. The Christian counselor sees in the counselee both the presence of the Kingdom of God in terms of the counselee's intrinsic worth as a child of God, and at the same time acknowledges that the Kingdom is not yet. The entrapment may be caused by society, the self or sin, to use Gutiérrez's distinctions.

Therefore there need to be three elements to a Christian counselor's analysis. Firstly, at base, there is the image of God's Kingdom and the image of God. Secondly, there are the counselor's theories about how people come to be trapped, and different theories about how the world operates. Finally, there is the ability to create a coherent whole or synthesis between the first two elements. This synthesis and the resultant consistency in counseling approach represents an ongoing conversion in the life of the counselor.

1. IMAGES OF GOD AND THE KINGDOM

In the previous chapter I discussed the importance for the counselor of his or her image of God. It should not be surprising, therefore, that this image also affects the counselor's ability to analyze the world. At its very simplest, the counselor with an individualist idea of God may even have difficulty seeing why it is necessary to analyze: all that is necessary is for the counselee to accept God, say, in the person of Jesus, and all problems will be solved. Such analysis, in so far as it occurs, tends to center on the question of why people don't or won't accept Jesus in this way, and the answer tends to be that the person is selfish or foolish — a sinner. Inadequate images of God lead to inadequate analysis.

Every image has its strengths and weaknesses for analysis. As the person moves towards a position where no image of God is necessary, while retaining images where they are appropriate, the person is increasingly able to grapple with the world as it is. The "world" can no longer threaten our image or faith in God. The pain of Auschwitz can be looked at, participated in, and borne: God is not dead, but our delusions are.

2. THEORIES ABOUT THE WORLD

The second element of Christian analysis — the use of different theories to understand the world — varies greatly from person to person and from situation to situation. Most people, even the least theoretical, have some ideas about how the world operates. (And, often, the least theoretical are the most definite in their ideas and their opinions!) We all need to operate on the basis of some theory so that we can predict with reasonable accuracy what is going to happen next in our lives. For instance, if we don't have a theory that tomorrow is going to be, in many ways, similar to today, then we will live in the midst of constant bewilderment, a barely tolerable state of being for an adult. A theory, in essence, is a series of ideas that we hope explains something.

The Christian counselor must account for and work with a plethora of theories: about the counselee and his or her place in the world, about his or her relationship to the counselor as well as about the nature of counseling itself. Some theories are very comprehensive, such as those of Freud, Marx and Darwin. Others are very specific, dealing with a particular aspect of behavior e.g. school refusal. Others, such as the various schools of family therapy, tend to cover the middle ground. What is certain is that no one counselor can hope to be conversant with every theory relevant to every counselee or every problem.

A lecturer I knew had the following maxim for his students: "It doesn't particularly matter which theory you use so long as you use one!" Like all maxims, that is somewhat of an oversimplification. However, it points to a couple of important truths: firstly, a theory gives us a frame of reference to think about phenomena in a consistent way, within the framework of the theory; secondly, all theories are limited because they do not describe all of reality, only a part.

In general terms, the better the theory, the more we can explain before being forced into inconsistency. Also, a sound theory should be able to predict. The better the theory the more accurate, comprehensive and long-lasting are the predictions. Good theory is also practical. Indeed, as Kurt Lewin has pointed out, "There is nothing so practical as good theory."

There are, of course, dangers in theory building. It is possible for us to get lost in our pet theory, and forget to check that our theory matches the world as we experience it. Marxism, for example, neglects the individual's psychology and causes many problems for young radicals. While Marxism is useful in some areas as an explanatory tool, like all theories, there are limits to its ability to explain all of reality. When these limits are not realized problems arise. Also, there is the problem of jargon. Certainly, when we are trying to explain complex phenomena, some specialist words are often helpful, but jargon misused can replace thought with its shadow. Finally, there is the problem of raising a theory to the status of an ideology. When this occurs the person mistakenly believes that the theory can explain all phenomena, and indeed for some people the theory and the world become one and the same.

The search for ever better explanatory theories is part of the search for truth. Truth, for the Christian, is one of the attributes of God. In a sense, then, sound theories about the world not only explain the world, but help to reveal aspects of God that were previously hidden or unknown. Developments in archaeology, astronomy, physics and biology (to name just a few) have greatly expanded the Christian's appreciation of God as creator. Earlier this century, the spirituality of Tielhard de Chardin was built on advances in science, and what was true of Chardin is now true of nearly every Christian in the developing West: the perception of God has been radically expanded by our advances in knowledge. However, most theories do not mention God by name, and indeed this is as it should be. God is never object, and cannot be objectified as just another factor among many.

When our images of the Kingdom of God and our theories of the world meet, there is often a clash. Perhaps either our ideas of the Kingdom of God are inadequate or our theories of the world's operation are inadequate. Or, finally and most seriously, the way that the world operates as revealed by our theories is seriously challenged by the Kingdom of God. An example here is the phenomenon of child abuse. Until the last few decades it was believed that this was a relatively rare phenomenon. Partly as a result of a great deal of research it has become apparent that it is, in fact, a large and serious problem affecting many children. That such practices of exploitation and betrayal of children can occur in our society cries out to God for action. The abuse of children is unimaginable in the Kingdom of God. Such a phenomenon challenges many an inadequate idea of God, and it also challenges the Christian to action.

3. SYNTHESIS AND CONVERSION

When our world view is challenged by the Kingdom of God, and we respond to this challenge, the response can most aptly be described as a conversion. Conversion is a complex term. A central concept in Christianity, and commonly used, it remains in many ways mysterious. People who as adults have become Christian often speak of a conversion experience. Those who were baptized as infants and brought up in a Christian household, though they may not experience the drama of an adult conversion, still participate in an ongoing conversion experience as they grow closer to God. As Gutiérrez points out, "All Christian life begins with a conversion, which means breaking with personal and social sin, and embarking on a new course."[1]

Such is the strength of the conversion experience that some mistakenly believe that we have only to experience this conversion to solve all our problems. Two theologians, James Fowler and Bernard Lonergan, give us a useful perspective on conversion.

For Fowler, conversion has to do with changes in the contents of faith. "Conversion is a significant recentering of one's previous conscious or unconscious images of value and power, and the conscious adoption of a new set of master stories in the commitment to reshape one's life in a new community of interpretation and action."[2] Conversion can occur in any of the faith stages discussed in an earlier chapter or in any of the transitions between them. There are significant advantages in thinking about conversion in the way that Fowler suggests.

Firstly, Fowler well describes the way many people reflect on their conversion experience. There is a feeling that the story of a person's life changes when a conversion occurs. The facts, such as being born on a certain date, as the son or daughter of certain parents, may remain, but the meanings that are attributed to these and all other events are totally altered. The story is changed, both in the past and the future as well as in the present. Secondly, Fowler emphasizes the commitment of conversion. It is not just an intellectual or cognitive event, but something that also redirects the will of the person in action.

Yet there is a limitation, which is that Fowler offers perhaps too static a view of conversion, not allowing for the continual conversion that Christians experience. Fowler makes clear that conversion should not be confused with progression through the stages of faith, which is another type of change. Because conversion is about changes in the content of faith, it does not of itself lead to growth through any of the stages of faith. The main impetus for change in Fowler's system is the developmental imperative, the internal contradictions that each stage creates, and certain pressures from the external environment. All this is helpful. The one dynamic that Fowler seems to have neglected is that of the continuing conversion experience.

Bernard Lonergan allows precisely for this ongoing dynamic. He comments that: "By conversion is understood a transformation of the subject and his world. Normally it is a prolonged process though its explicit acknowledgment may be concentrated in a few momentous judgements and decisions."[3] Interestingly, Lonergan agrees with Fowler that conversion "is not just a development or a series of developments. Rather it is a resultant change of course and direction."[4] Lonergan then goes on to describe how conversion, though intensely personal, can also be communal and historical, can spread from one culture to another and can adapt to changing circumstances and epochs. Conversion therefore affects all of a person's conscious and intentional operations. It directs the gaze, pervades the imagination, releases the symbols that penetrate to the depths of the psyche. It enriches understanding, guides judgements, reinforces decisions. At a communal and historical level, conversion encourages a reflection that explores its origins, developments, purposes, achievements and failures.[5]

Another concept that Lonergan develops that can aid our understanding of conversion is "horizon." Using as his starting point the literal sense of the word horizon, meaning the bounding circle, the line at which earth and sky appear to meet, Lonergan argues that the scope of our knowledge and the range of our interests are also bounded by a metaphorical or analogous horizon. "In this sense what lies beyond one's horizon is simply outside the range of one's knowledge and interests: one neither knows or cares. But what lies within one's horizon is in some measure, great or small, an object of interest and of knowledge."[6] A conversion is a change from one horizon to another that involves an about-face in the person making the change. It is a new order that repudiates certain characteristics of the old horizon and which, Lonergan argues, reveals ever greater depth, and breadth and wealth.[7]

The conversion experience is pivotal to the Christian ability to analyze society. This experience, we have seen, is not just a one-off event but an ongoing process of renewal, which can even be transmitted from one generation in the family to the next. My three year old participates in my conversion experience and then, in her life, may carry on that experience to an ever greater depth, breadth and wealth as Lonergan puts it. I participated in a dramatic conversion experience of my mother's which changed her life quite radically, and which, in turn, helped to shape my life in faith and my conversion experience. Hence, my daughter participates in the conversion of her grandmother, whom she never actually knew. It is possible in some families to go back a number of generations before reaching a truly dramatic conversion event. The children, of course, will not necessarily use the conversion process to go deeper than their parents. If they become stuck at the level of their parents, religion quickly becomes a security blanket that supports the status quo. The newness of the conversion experience is lost, and the radical encounter with God becomes formalized, a mere shadow of what could be possible. Such Christians tend to accept the prevailing societal norms as though they were God given. They become stuck in the world as it was for them as children, never realizing that this world was in a large part a creation of their parents' and their generation.

Similarly, groups that are converted tend, over time, to rise in socio-economic class. This is due to some of the secondary effects of conversion, such as greater care of family, seeing work as meaningful and not dissipating energy in a constant struggle to escape reality by using alcohol, drugs and other dysfunctional methods. Often, to be born into a comfortable middle-class family makes it harder to relate to a God who identifies so closely with the poor and dispossessed. Also, if parents cease to deepen their own faith as adults, this acts as a role model for children and gives the message to the child that neither faith nor conversion are dynamic life events.

However, if the conversion process is not thwarted, there is a constantly exciting dynamic as we enter, in effect, ever deeper into the horizon of Christ. It is no wonder, then, that conversion is an ongoing process, rather than a one off event. Given the moral, psychological and emotional mess most of us are in when we are converted, it is not surprising that most people at their initial conversion can only catch a glimpse of this horizon, and yet this glimpse is a staggering life changing event. It takes years and perhaps generations before people can say with confidence with Paul, "But we are those who have the mind of Christ." (1 Cor 2:16) Even so, Paul warns that in this life, "we are seeing a dim reflection in a mirror": "through a glass darkly" (1 Cor 13:12), as the King James Bible puts it more poetically. The dim reflection is, however, more real than anything else that we experience, for in this reflection we begin to see the world as Christ sees it — not just cognitive knowledge, but a gift that flows from our response to the loving relationship of the Trinity. Our whole person is involved as we look at the world in the outflowing of Divine love. At the same time, we are shaken to our roots by the Divine sorrow and suffering, and we begin to see the terrible consequences of the world's and our own failure to love.

Our ongoing conversion means we are committed to enter ever deeper into this Divine mystery and love. As we do so, God challenges the parts of our lives that do not conform with the image of God revealed in the ongoing conversion and that do not conform to the image of the world which is in the mind of Christ. If we accept the challenge as an act of a loving God, then we can be said to be dying to self. Out of this death which participates in Christ's death, there is an ever deepening love. The love is not just a mystical event between ourselves and God, but an event that takes place in the world in an outflowing of practical and emotional love for the people about us and the whole creation.

CONVERSION AND ACTION

Our analysis of the world, then, is transformed by ongoing conversion. Earlier, I referred to the need for a synthesis of our image of God and our theories about the world. It is in our conversion that this synthesis takes place. Without conversion, an analysis lacks life and depth, for it leaves out the self, and ultimately it leaves out God. It is by conversion that a Christian is able to be both in the world and not of it. It is by conversion that the Christian is able to maintain a perspective, in the mind of Christ, that encourages Christian analysis. We can consider various theories and appreciate their truth and use their truth to challenge inadequate images of God. At the same time, the same theories can point to aspects of the world that are challenged by the Christian images of God and the vision of the Kingdom of God that is already forming. In both these clashes, action is called for; an action which is, primarily, Christian conversion — a cognitive, emotional and religious event that has immediate practical consequences. In conversion, both the person and the world are changed.

[1] Gutiérrez, Gustavo, "Theology and the Social Sciences, [1984]", in Gutiérrez, Gustavo, *The Truth Shall Make You Free*, Orbis Books, Maryknoll, New York, 1990, p.56.
[2] Fowler, James W., *Stages of Faith: The Psychology of Human Development and the Quest for Meaning*, Collins Dove, Blackburn, 1989, pp.281-282.
[3] Lonergan, Bernard, *Method in Theology*, Darton, Longman & Todd, London, 1972, p.130.
[4] id.
[5] ibid., pp.130-131.
[6] ibid., p.236
[7] ibid., pp.235-238.

6

Practice Application: Counseling and Child Abuse

In this chapter, I will attempt to show how images of God and theories of counseling can be applied in the treatment of child abuse. I have chosen the field of child abuse for three reasons: firstly, it is an area in which I have some experience as a counselor; secondly, as a problem, child abuse can be notoriously difficult to treat, so it is useful to test the insights that I have previously discussed to see if they shed further light or give direction in solving what are in effect some of counseling's hard cases; thirdly, the child who is abused is in some ways the paradigm of all counselees. All counselees share the abused child's need to be liberated from what entraps them and diminishes them as a person.

DEFINITIONAL PROBLEMS

Child abuse is not a simple phenomenon that we can readily identify. How people define "abuse" depends on many factors, such as, for example, their position in society. A judge is likely to define abuse differently to a doctor, a taxi-driver to a bureaucrat, a captain of industry to a laborer. There are also numbers of different definitions of abuse that get written down or otherwise institutionalized. A child protection agency may have one definition or set of criteria that differs markedly from guidelines, say, in the education department. While it would be helpful if all such definitions were compatible, the reality is that often they are not. Also, even when definitions exist, they tend to remain vague and open to different interpretations: when, say, does corporal punishment become abuse? Also, within the general term of "abuse," how do we distinguish various types of abuse? Though we often categorize abuse as physical, sexual, psychological/emotional or neglect, this is not the only typology, nor always the most useful. While we discuss definitional problems, it is important not to forget that even what we mean by "child" can also change over time and from culture to culture.

And, yet, even if we could satisfactorily define the term, we would only have begun to understand the phenomenon of abuse. We need, as well, to understand the internal dynamics of abuse in the individual and the family, its relationship to society and culture, its causes and effects and a host of other factors: it is in this confused context that the Christian counselor has to discern what he or she can offer.

FIRST CONTACT: THE FAMILY HORIZON AND CHRISTIAN CONVERSION

Debates about definitions, however, are too theoretical for most counselors when they first come across the phenomenon they may, later, call child abuse. At their first close encounter with child abuse, what they commonly experience are feelings of alarm, if not panic — not a clear cognitive event. Such a reaction is as true for child protection officers on a home visit or for psychiatrists in a consulting room as for neighbors over the back fence. I well remember my own first experience. As a social worker employed by a local authority, I visited a house where there had been an anonymous report of abuse to a child. In retrospect, I must have given a stirling impression of counselor as stunned mullet — mind blurred, heart pounding, my feet turned to lead, my tongue frozen in my mouth. Fortunately, I was accompanied by an experienced counselor who managed to conduct the interview (albeit with a fish under her arm).

A counselor's vulnerability at first contact with child abuse is important. It is foundational to an understanding of the phenomenon of child abuse. There are a number of factors which generate alarm and panic, such as inexperience, probable conflict of roles, performance anxiety and perhaps fear of violence. However, at another level, the counselor's feelings mirror the experiences of the child and the family. We enter the emotional horizon of the family. We enter into the feeling world of the family, with all its limitations and turbulence. This entry into the family horizon is necessary if we are to gain real empathy with the people in the situation, even if we feel overwhelmed. Children who are abused and their families live in a frightening world whose horizon has nightmare dimensions. In this world they feel trapped and powerless.

Not only does the Christian counselor enter the horizon of the other but he/she is converted by the experience. In the horizon of the other is the suffering horizon of Christ. Gutiérrez argues that, as each person is the living temple of God, we meet God in our encounter with people as they live in the world,[1] and that this is especially true of our encounters with the poor.[2] In contact with child abuse, we not only experience the pain of a child or of a family, but also the pain of Christ.

Many recoil from this pain, this conversion, this death to self, and build all manner of defensive structures to protect themselves: "the child asked for it" (broken bones); "the five year old was seductive" (to her father who molested her); "we can't interfere with the family"; "parents have rights" (but no talk of responsibilities). Each of these responses (and others) can be potent means of protecting us from the pain which is the reality of child abuse. Such pain threatens our illusions about self and others, and about the society in which we live and on which we depend.

When we enter another's horizon, we enter not only into the horizon of Christ, but also into a horizon that is structured in part by values that are destructive, that are not life giving: in other words, by values of evil. This is more marked in child abuse cases, but is true whenever we enter another's horizon, for no-one is entirely free of evil. Entering another's horizon is dangerous. It is possible to be overpowered by destructiveness. The counselor may find him/herself acting out the violence that is found in the family — expressing anger at the child for being a "bad" child, at the family for being a bad family, at the other professionals involved for being bad professionals. The counselor may get caught up in the family's deceit that effectively hides their acts of abuse from themselves, or the counselors may even turn the evil on themselves, become depressed and lose their own sense of self worth. Change cannot occur if the counselor is incapacitated by the evil of the other's horizon.

The situation is further complicated because the counselor's own horizon is also in part structured by the values of evil. No one of us, counselors included, is ever totally free from such structures that we inherit from our culture and society, from our family of origin and early experiences, and from our own actions. The counselor may not perceive, or may mistakenly perceive, the horizon of the other, especially where evil is unconscious, and most is. (Ps 19:12)

Some years ago, a colleague said to me, commenting on a serious physical abuse case that had been referred to him, "I don't understand why there is all this fuss. I often leave similar bruises on my own child." A somewhat extreme example, perhaps, but it does reflect the truth that counselors who have legitimated their own faults have difficulty perceiving those faults in others. Furthermore, where faults are denied rather than legitimated by the counselor, there is the danger that similar faults in counselees will be exaggerated or, in some cases when they don't actually exist in the counselee, imagined. Psychoanalysts call this phenomenon projection. We don't have to work in the counseling field for too long before we come across the angry counselor, who is always diagnosing anger in counselees, or creating angry counselees. Whether faults are denied or legitimated, a conversion needs to take place in the counselor before he or she can be of assistance to the counselee. Otherwise the counselor will be incapable of understanding that part of the person's horizon that is most in need of change, and the counselor's own problems will distort any perspective of the other's horizon.

Actual failings by the counselor are not the only impediments to entering the horizon of the counselee. Even where the failing of the counselee is not reflected in actuality in the counselor, there is still the potential for the counselor to fail in a similar manner: there but for the Grace of God go I. However, this realization is often as threatening as real faults. Can we imagine ourselves sexually abusing a child, for instance? Such thoughts can disturb the sense of self-concept and the illusions about personal goodness and self-sufficiency. Given different circumstances, most of us can imagine ourselves doing unspeakable deeds. Because the gap between our path and the abyss of moral bankruptcy is not so great, there is extra urgency to that plea in the Lord's prayer, "Do not put us to the test!" Most of us know that, were we put to the test, we would fail, and we come to realize the absolute necessity of God's grace.

GRACE AND SIN: IN HOPE OF FREEDOM

Grace is not heavenly money stored in a divine bank account, so that when the account is in the black we are okay, and when the account is in the red we are in trouble. Such an understanding of grace locates it outside our relationship with God, whereas grace is much more to do with the liberating presence of God in our lives. When we know that we are trapped, and are unable to free ourselves by our own efforts, then we are in need of grace. Trapped and then freed, we experience grace. This is the experience of the Jews as they are freed from the oppression of Egypt, and liberated from the institutionalised child abuse of Pharaoh: "Pharaoh then gave his subjects this command: 'Throw all the boys born to the Hebrews into the river, but let all the girls live.'" (Ex 1:22) God saves Moses specifically from such a death through the intervention of Pharaoh's daughter, and later Moses becomes the one through whom God liberates the Hebrews. Moses, in his role of liberator, prefigures Jesus, whose birth is also marked by the institutionalized killing of children, as the forces of evil seek to destroy a threat to their power. " . . . In Bethlehem and its surrounding district he [Herod] had all the male children killed who were two years old or under. . . ." The juxtaposition of the story of the birth of Jesus and the murder of the innocents highlights the opposition between grace and sin. Jesus, the liberator, comes to bring life in the midst of a world where oppression brings death.[3]

What do we mean by being "trapped," and what is it that we need to be freed from? The traditional Christian answer is "sin." However, the notion of sin is not simple: we are not talking here of sin as transgression against a personal moral code, but of sin as both what stops us acting in accordance with God's will by unjustly limiting our freedom, and also our specific failures to act in accordance with that will. The first is experienced as the sin of others and society, and the second is experienced as our own personal sin. As I am using the terms, sin and evil could be synonyms, and henceforth I will use them interchangeably.

That we are able not to transgress a moral code (perhaps the Ten Commandments), does not free us from sin or evil. Clearly, it does not free us from the evil meted out to us by others or by society. The inmates of Auschwitz still experienced evil no matter how faithful they were to their moral code. Following a moral code did not free them from the pain and the constriction of the external evil. Similarly, we often see young abused children trying heroically to be "good." Their efforts are to no avail, and the injustice of abuse seems to pursue them relentlessly. In both cases there needs to be liberation beyond the moral code. There needs to be grace.

At a personal level, we as counselors are usually all too aware of our own limited abilities to care and to love. Exhortations to pull ourselves up by our moral bootstraps are of little use, because so often when we look at our lives, we see that we consistently do the thing that we do not wish to do. This is something that St. Paul well knew:

> In fact, this seems to be the rule, that every single time I want to do good it is something evil that comes to hand. In my inmost self I dearly love God's Law, but I can see that my body follows a different law that battles against the law that my reason dictates. This is what makes me a prisoner of that law which lives inside my body. (Rom 7:21-23)

Paul asks: "Who will rescue me from this body doomed to death?" (Rom 7:24) And he answers: "Thanks be to God through Jesus Christ our Lord." (Rom 7:25) Paul does not just say "God" but "God through Jesus Christ," recognizing the centrality of the theme of liberation in the life and teaching of Jesus. The power of evil will not ultimately triumph over me, for, though its power is greater than mine and its presence influences me to do evil, through Jesus I am reunited in relationship with the Father. Grace then is far more than a commodity. Grace is the liberating presence of God through Christ.

The Christian concepts of sin and grace have important implications for the counseling of child abuse cases. As a Christian, the counselor can be confident that no evil is so great or powerful that it can reverse the final liberation of

Christ. Jesus himself describes this graphically when he says, "I watched Satan fall like lightning from heaven." (Luke 10:18) At the same time, the counselor is also aware that the power of evil persists and at times even seems to triumph, as in the execution of Jesus. We cannot magically banish evil, but evil can be overcome by love, a love that is vulnerable, a love that is at the heart of God. Though Jesus was himself killed, his faithfulness to God's loving will endured, and in this loving faithfulness Jesus announces a new Kingdom of Liberation. The treatment of child abuse needs to be seen within this perspective of the ongoing liberation of Christ. It is the liberation of the child, of the family, of the counselor and of the society. The counselor is both the recipient of liberating grace, but also the means by which the other as child, family or society experiences such grace.

Neil Ormerod believes that our understanding of grace and sin must go together.[4] As our understanding of one concept increases, so does our knowledge of the other. At the same time he warns that: "At some point an account of the origins of evil must break down since, in fact, evil has no 'origin,' no cause. It will always confront us with a mystery which has no full explanation."[5] Ormerod goes on to say that there is a danger in so intellectualizing evil that it comes to be seen as reasonable. While grace can abound in every situation, evil is never reasonable nor something which we need to accommodate. Ultimately, there can never be a theoretical solution to evil, but only "a practical solution of living in God's forgiving grace."[6] This then needs to be the stance of the counselor when confronted by the reality of the evil of child abuse in the other and at least its potential in him or herself. Great though the suffering, there is always the hope of the loving liberation of God, even when children die, or when children are condemned to years of torment.

The Christian counselor is free to enact this freedom, this grace. Although a counselor is not always effective in changing the external or internal structures of evil, the Christian counselor, in carrying out God's providential will, does not have to accommodate evil. What this means in practice is that the counselor is free to enter into the suffering of the other, to share at a deep level the fate of the victim, and in this sharing not to be overcome by evil. Impossible though it is, this is the method of Jesus, and only in so far as we enter the life of Jesus, can we achieve it. At this level real change can occur, a real liberation may take place.

It also at this level that the counselor leaves him or herself open to the tremendous desolation of seeing the unreasonable suffering of children one knows and loves — suffering that, worse still, the counselor may be powerless to change. There is never any guarantee that a Christian counselor will be effective in correcting injustice. Indeed, at this point in our knowledge of the treatment of child abuse, failures are likely to outnumber successes, and the small gains we make need to be seen against the background of an ocean of hurt. Margaret Lynch, the former president of the International Society for the Prevention of Child Abuse and Neglect, commented a few years ago that the amount of pain a worker feels "deepens rather than lessens with time and experience."[7]

What then saves us from despair? If the work is so difficult and the results so uncertain, why bother doing it? Christian counselors who work in the field of child abuse have one legitimate reason for doing so: they are called by God, and their work is part of God's providential will. While there may well be other mediating variables that draw them into the field, such as psychological, emotional or structural factors, ultimately the legitimation is the call from God. To work in any field, if it is not part of God's providential will, is a waste of time — if not a disaster — no matter how talented the worker may be. The Christian counselor who is called to the field has no choice if he or she desires to do what God requires. Freedom, for the Christian counselor, is obedience to God's call, and hope must rest on God's promise that we are never asked for more than we are able to give, and that in doing God's will we are in effect participating in the work of God. Faith and grace and hope do not allow the Christian counselor to evade reality, but orient us ever more forcibly towards it. Ultimately, there are no illusions, no projections, no denials, no fantasies. We have to tackle the problems of child abuse with all the pain and the complexities. Every skill and every resource that the counselor can muster needs to be mobilized in this striving for change, and central to this striving is compassion.

COMPASSION AS UNCONDITIONAL LOVE

Anuradha Vittachi, in an account of the work of Archbishop Desmond Tutu, writes:

> Tutu's faith and belief in the importance in meeting the needs of the marginalized demands a pro-active involvement: "When the Spirit of the Lord is upon you, watch out! Because it does not allow you to luxuriate in a spiritual ghetto, a kind of ivory tower. The Spirit of the Lord propels you into the world God loved."
>
> Just what can a clergyman do, though? Faced with the terrible tragedies that occur everyday in the shanty-towns fringing the cities, where millions of black and "colored" people live to provide cheap labor for the elite in the city centres, it is easy for a pastor to feel helpless. And feeling helpless is a deeply distressing experience.

But Tutu seems open to the experience — and even to admitting frankly to its pain. For example, he described to us his attempt to comfort a mother whose sons, aged 11 and 13, had been pulled out of their house and shot arbitrarily by the police: "She sat there in front of us, and kept wiping her eyes — but there were no more tears. It seemed as if she were trying to remove from in front of her face the images she couldn't bear to look on. I've never felt such a fraud, trying to tell her about the love of God...."

Compassion at its toughest and truest is said to be the ability to "be with suffering" (compassion) when there seems no way out of the pain. This is the challenge that Tutu accepts: to remain present, with a never-ending offer of love and hope, when there appears to be no cause for anything but despair — without running away.

Tutu takes the passion of Jesus as his guiding light. His parishioners' humiliation, abandonment, arrest, torture, despair, death are all paralleled in Jesus' Good Friday experience. But since Jesus, Tutu believes, miraculously rose on Easter Sunday ("breaking the bonds of death"), why should we not feel hope also for new life and freedom for his people?[8]

We see the mobilizing principle of Desmond Tutu's life, an horizon open to Christ's suffering and open to the suffering of the other. Though powerless, and in his own words, a "fraud" at one level, Tutu has compassion, a burning awesome power that is oriented to the good. More than empathy, this is a pathos that rushes from the center of being itself, from beyond objects, from the subjective relationship of the Trinity. And pathos is an active enabler. As Desmond Tutu rightly says, "Watch out!" Through empathy we "feel with" and even "understand with." But compassion pushes us further, to feel and understand at the level at which the other is loved by God. This "feeling with," this "understanding with," calls us into a radical solidarity with the counselee. We can no longer be neutral, impartial, value free. In Bernard Lonergan's terms, compassion has sublimited empathy. We are committed in love.

In a compassionate relationship, we are not subsumed or overwhelmed by the other. Rather, we are given greater clarity of vision. Beyond the myths of scientific objectivity, the counselor glimpses the perspective of God — the horizon that both affirms and challenges all other horizons, including that of the counselor and the counselee. In the counseling relationship, the counselee has infinite worth, but also has an horizon terribly damaged by sin and evil. The compassionate perspective commits the counselor to adopt as honest an appraisal of the counselee as he or she is capable of. Furthermore, the counselor sees that, in the horizon of Christ, his or her own horizon and immediate destiny are linked inextricably to that of the counselee. Their pathos is shared, and there is a drive to free the other from the limitations of a constricted horizon, by making real the horizon of Christ through sharing.

Importantly, the counselor's horizon is not the horizon of Christ because, inevitably, we fall short. Tutu's comment, "I have never felt such a fraud in my life," is familiar to all sensitive counselors in the child abuse field. We are all frauds, and our limitations and failings contribute to the problems that we are trying to solve.

Yet our fraudulence is not fatal. When we recognize it, we are able to understand at a deeper level, a level that resonates in us the entrapment of the other. Failing to recognize our limitations and shortcomings has potentially disastrous consequences in counseling relationships. Some years ago, a slightly obese colleague had the unenviable task of taking children from inebriated parents and removing them to a place of safety. In a moment of exasperation, my colleague said to the mother, "Why the hell do you drink so much?" To which the mother replied, "For the same f..king reason you eat too much!" Real compassion occurs when such mutual entrapment is recognized. It is at this point of entrapment, as we have noted before, that there is the potential for liberating grace — and the point at which conversion can occur.

CONVERSION RECONSIDERED

Conversion, as we have seen, is a radical shifting of horizons. For the victim of child abuse, this conversion can mean the emergence of genuine hope that life will no longer be constrained by acts of abuse, and the birth of a self-esteem that is fundamentally unshakable. For the perpetrator of abuse there is a similar experience. But, because evil has trapped this individual even more thoroughly — it is well documented for instance, that often the perpetrator of abuse was him or herself a victim of abuse — there is an even greater liberation. The perpetrator is no longer controlled by the compulsion to harm, but can begin to act differently and put an end to the abuse.

Conversion, then, is a process. When conversion occurs, we should not expect that all abuse necessarily stops, that all wounds are healed. Rather, conversion marks the beginning of a process in a new direction, a journey with a new horizon. Often, especially in serious abuse cases, there needs to be a series of conversions if change is to continue.

Society, too, can turn back from child abuse and experience a conversion. The work of Henry Kempe and his colleagues in alerting the world to the problem of child abuse, and the response that work has received, has marked a conversion for society. Like all conversions it was partial at first with the release of the historic article, "The Battered-Child Syndrome."[9] But gradually that conversion was followed by others: the growth of the International Society for the Prevention of Child Abuse and Neglect; the growing recognition of sexual and emotional abuse, and lately the recognition of the abuse of children in the Third World and the part that the developed world plays in that process. As with nearly all conversions, it is patchy. At times motives are ambiguous, and the structures of evil persist. Yet the horizon of a substantial part of the world has changed over the last thirty years as a result of this ongoing conversion.

It should be apparent that conversion goes beyond popular piety and a simplistic "accepting Jesus into your heart." Although conversion occurs when we open ourselves to the horizon of Christ, it does not necessarily follow that we need to express this conversion in the language of the institutional church. As Christians, we have so failed in our calling that for many, especially those who have been abused, the language of the church is not the sign of liberation, but of bondage and torment. William Blake has expressed this dilemma most ably in the poem "The Little Vagabond."

> Dear Mother, dear Mother, the church is cold,
> But the Ale-house is healthy & pleasant & warm;
> Besides I can tell where I am used well,
> Such usage in heaven will never do well.
> But if at the church they would give us some Ale,
> And a pleasant fire our souls to regale,
> We'd sing and we'd pray all the live-long day,
> Nor ever once wish from the Church to stray.

For people such as the little vagabond, church language is incomprehensible. Yet they have an intuitively correct insight that, if God exists, then God meets them at their greatest and most human need. If we as counselors are to talk of God, it must be by using the language of the counselee's experience — in effect, the language of God. Yet paradoxically, the word "God" for the counselee in distress is often either meaningless or oppressive. Think for an instance of the child who was sexually abused by a trusted religious teacher. What connotations does the word "God" have for that person?

We underestimate God when we come to believe that God can only achieve conversion in ways that we have come to expect as normal, or by using language with which we are comfortable. God calls Christians to participate in the ongoing work of conversion, but the work does not stop when they fail to take up the challenge. Conversion can take place in seemingly secular movements. I have already noted the movement to alert the world to the problems of child abuse. The environmental and feminist movements are other examples of liberation where God's grace and conversion are present.

To understand conversion as an historical and societal as well as an individual process, gives a greater depth to our understanding of the Kingdom of God. This understanding of conversion heals the split in many Christians' thinking when we come to consider our work in the world with other men and women of good will. Too often we feel that our work would be more real if we could only introduce the other, be it colleague, counselee or society, to Christ. "If only the other would be converted," the Christian thinks, and this conversion is understood in a rather narrow sense of the word. But an expanded notion of conversion would suggest that conversion is already occurring, in so far as the other — be it colleague, counselee or society — has taken on the horizon of Christ. The fact that they do not use "church" words is immaterial. Some counselees will find "church" words quite useful in understanding the changes which occur in counseling; many will not.

What is important is that a conversion is now occurring. In this conversion something new is happening. The Kingdom of God is breaking through the structures of evil. In so far as the Christian counselor is tuned into his or her own conversion, and is open to further conversion, the Christian counselor will be able to tune into the other's conversion and facilitate further change. Hence, the Christian counselor is fully able to throw him or herself into the work, and in so doing help bring about the Kingdom of God — without perhaps ever mentioning the name of God or Christ. What is important is that our work is sensitive to our own conversion experience and hence the horizon of Christ, and that we too are sensitive to this horizon breaking through in those around us.

Finally, we need also to be sensitive to the structures of evil that impede the breaking through process. Such sensitivity will guide the choice of counseling methods used by the counselor, which is the subject of the next chapter.

---

[1] Gutiérrez, Gustavo, *A Theology of Liberation*, Orbis Books, Maryknoll, New York, 1973, p.194.
[2] Gutiérrez, Gustavo, "A Discussion of Gustavo Gutiérrez's Work [Lyons, 1985]," *The Truth Shall Make You Free: Confrontations*, Orbis Books, Maryknoll, New York, 1990, p.5.

[3] Gutiérrez, Gustavo, *The God of Life,* Orbis Books, Maryknoll, New York, 1991. p.3.
[4] Ormerod, Neil, *Grace and Disgrace: A Theology of Self-Esteem, Society and History,* E.J. Dwyer, Newtown, 1992.
[5] ibid., p.146.
[6] id.
[7] Lynch, Margaret, "The International Society for Prevention of Child Abuse and Neglect: The Future." *Child Abuse and Neglect,* 1986, 10, p.452.
[8] Vittachi, Anuradha, "Just call me Arch", *The New Internationalist,* July 1992, No 233. p.35.
[9] Kempe, C. Henry, Silverman, Frederic N., Steele, Brandt F., Droegemueller, William, Silver, Henry K., "The Battered-Child Syndrome", *Journal of the American Medical Association,* July 7, 1962, 181:17-24,.

Christian Theology and Understanding of Methods of Counseling

A COMMON METHODOLOGY

By exploring the relationship between spirituality and theological method, the liberation theologian, Gustavo Gutiérrez, suggests insights that can enrich our discussion of the relationship between theology and counseling method. Gutiérrez argues that:

> In the book that tells of the Acts of the first Christian community, the Christian manner of life is given a particular and original name: "the way." The word is used without any further qualification. To "follow the way" means to conduct oneself in a certain manner; the Greek *hodos* can mean both conduct and way or path. Christians are distinguished by their behavior, their lifestyle. This sets the community apart in both the Jewish and the pagan worlds in which it lives and bears witness. Its behavior consists in a way of thinking and acting, of walking according to the spirit. (see Rom. 8:4)[1]

For Gutiérrez, if one is to be a Christian the course to follow is the same course along which one must move in order to theologize. The methodology of the Christian theologian is his or her spirituality, that is, his or her way of being Christian. The Christian theologian reflects on the mystery of God by following in the footsteps of Jesus. By walking with the Spirit, he or she proclaims the love freely bestowed by the Father on every human being.[2]

Using the same logic as Gutiérrez, I believe that the Christian counselor's methodology is his or her spirituality.

It follows that the methodology of the Christian counselor is also the methodology of the theologian. Yet the methods of the two are not necessarily the same. A biblical scholar, for instance, translates and interprets recently found papyri of the Old Testament using different methods to the counselor working with a couple experiencing marital problems. Methodology is an overarching term that describes the totality of methods in a particular field and that abstracts their commonality. Gutiérrez claims that the methodology of theology is primarily a "way," a following of Christ. Similarly, I claim that Christian counseling and theology are one and the same "way."

SQUARING METHODOLOGY AND METHOD

Both theologian and Christian counselor face difficult questions about how their methodology squares with the methods they use to carry out their work. The various methods we use derive from the socio/cultural context in which we work, of which only a part is explicitly Christian, and only part "converted." Attempting to achieve consistency between methodology and method, the theologian and the Christian counselor both need criteria by which they can judge their methods.

Liberation theologians have given a great deal of thought to the relationship of theology with the social sciences in general, and the theory and method of Marxism in particular. The approach has not simply been to appropriate that which seems superficially useful, but to enter deeply into a dialog that tries to clarify the extent to which both Marxism and sociology enter into the horizon of Christ within the South American context. A criterion and the methodological starting point for liberation theologians is the non-person. In the words of Gutiérrez:

> . . . in Latin America the challenge does not come first and foremost from non-believers

but from no-persons — that is, those whom the prevailing social order does not acknowledge as persons: the poor, the exploited, those systematically and lawfully stripped of their human status, those who hardly know what a human being is. Non-persons represent a challenge, not primarily to our religious world, but to our economic, social, political and cultural world: their existence is a call to revolutionary transformation of the very foundation of our dehumanizing society.

In this context, then, the question is not: How are we to talk of God in a world come of age?, but: How are we to proclaim God as a Father in a non-human world? What is implied when we tell non-persons that they are sons and daughters of God? . . .

In other words, the question being raised today in Latin America is: How can we speak of God in the face of the suffering of the innocent? . . . We can in fact claim that a language for speaking about God is rising among us today out of the unjust sufferings, but also the hopes, of the poor of Latin America.[3]

Let us apply this to the world of counseling where the starting point is the counselee. We judge all methods and approaches in relationship to this person. In our society we can usefully think of the counselee who seriously desires change as being poor in spirit. Counselees to some degree realize that they are not self-sufficient, and that, at a basic level, they are in need. Their whole being cries out for assistance. Furthermore, before receiving help, counselees often experience themselves as nonpersons at one or a variety of levels: as a result of direct exploitation, as in the case of abuse or racism; or due to a lack of care as in cases of neglect; or due to structural pressures such as unemployment. We can see, therefore, that the starting point of Christian counseling and one strand of theology, i.e. liberation theology, are very similar and, in some circumstances, the same.

METHOD AS DYNAMIC

There is no scientific method as such, but the vital feature of the scientist's procedure has been merely to do his utmost, no holds barred.[4]

Often when people talk of method they envisage something that is dry and abstract. This can certainly not be the case with Christian counseling. On the contrary, the process must be and is so dynamic it is hard to talk about method at all without confusion. Christian counseling requires that we use not only the mind but the whole person so that method leads to liberation. Here, "no holds barred" signifies creativity, enthusiasm and energy. For the Christian counselor, insights from any method are valid, provided they lead to a liberation to love. Methods are not rejected because they fail to measure up to some legalistic, dogmatic or moralistic criteria, but only because they are ineffective tools of genuine liberation.

The process of liberation is not one from which the Christian counselor can be distant and aloof. A starting point for the Christian counselor is that he/she too is a person with unfulfilled needs, a self in need of liberation, not a good righteous person who is so strong that they stand apart from the human condition to improve the lot of others. Further, the counselor's liberation is inextricably tied to the liberation of the counselee. As Desmond Tutu has pointed out, "Freedom, Sir, is indivisible."[5] Christian counselors, as others, are trapped by external and internal structures of evil, and they desperately need God and other people. The counselor and the counselee travel together in a joint exodus from entrapment to liberation. Though the counselor may have many talents and learned skills, these alone cannot save him or her, or others. Ultimately, liberation is a free gift from God which we agree to accept as part of God's providential plan or will for us.

Because the counseling relationship is a joint journey of liberation, the Christian counselor needs to be sensitive to what God is saying through the counselee. God can work through anyone whose ability to respond is not completely crippled by evil, even through the most psychotic and neurotic of counselees. Well or ill, we can all participate in God's action in the world, and while most mentally ill people would prefer to be well, just as would most physically ill people, their illness does not preclude them from being part of God's action. Only sin does.

PRAYER

It is inconceivable that a Christian counselor would not need and want to pray. Prayer is the conscious linking of the counselor with God and part of the means by which the counselor is attuned to the will of God. It is also the channel by which the counselor activates the power of God. It is the means by which the love of God can be made known, especially in harrowing and distressing situations in which all hope seems lost. It is a means by which God challenges the counselor to look at his/her own behavior, prejudices and faults. (Psalm 19:12) It is the means by which the counselor joins in the joyfulness, thankfulness and creativity of God.

Prayer is an integral part of the life of the Christian. Prayer and faith go together. There are different types of prayer, and generally a Christian will pray in a variety of different ways, depending on circumstances. With regard to counseling, the basic prayer is "God's will be done," or "God's providential plan be realised." In most instances, however, it is not appropriate to share prayer with the counselee. While shared prayer at the appropriate time is a powerful way of being open to God's presence, used inappropriately, it can be manipulative and destructive.

COMPREHENSIVE METHOD AND INTEGRAL LIBERATION

The Christian counselor is aware of the enormous range of people and conditions a counselee needs to depend on in order to live a fulfilled life: family, friends, colleagues and acquaintances; the social world with all its varied aspects; the media; the political, the economic and the artistic life. Finally, counselor and counselee alike depend on the physical world itself; the air, the water, the land, the trees and the animals. As counselors and counselees, we are part of an intricate web, and we depend on it for survival. Underpinning each of these relationships is the relationship with God. The concept of rugged individualism, fully realized, would lead to instantaneous death. As we saw in Chapter Three, liberation for the Christian counselor is an integral liberation. It is the liberation to enter more deeply into a loving relationship at every level of human existence. In successful counseling from the Christian perspective, there is at least a three-way reciprocal relationship. The counselor, the counselee and God each give, and each in turn receives. Together they create a new reality, and change occurs in all three. The new relationship, in so far as it is life giving, is incorporated into the life of the Trinity.

There is no one individual method that, by itself, is able to achieve integral liberation. Various methods can achieve aspects of this liberation. Some are more useful than others. All methods have shortcomings, as well as strengths.

One of the dangers for counselors is that they come to

rely on only one method or technique, and so forget that any method is secondary to the needs of the counselee. For the Christian, especially, any technique or method is simply a tool. The method does not explain the world or give it meaning. A good method can certainly provide insights into processes that were previously hidden — for example, the Freudian theory and the unconscious; behaviorism and conditioning — but none gives a total picture, or is all encompassing. Though this may seem self-evident, in practice methods can become a total world view for counselors. When this occurs, the counselor ceases to be open to information coming from the counselee that does not fit the method and its underlying theory. There is then the danger that the counseling relationship will break down, or, worse still, that the counselee will be pressured into giving responses that fit the counselor's theory and method. Counselors need to fit the method to the person, not vice versa.

CRITERIA TO DISCRIMINATE BETWEEN METHODS

Christians need to know how to discriminate between sound and unsound methods, useful and not so useful methods, the appropriate and not so appropriate. In order to discriminate, the Christian counselor needs criteria by which to judge the various methods. I suggest that there are five useful criteria: compatibility with the needs of the counselee; the degree to which change brings about freedom to love; the degree of respect for the counselee as person; the degree of respect for the interrelatedness of reality, and effectiveness.

1. Compatibility with the Needs of the Counselee

As we have already pointed out, the starting point for Christian counseling is our counselees and the needs that bring them to counseling. The particular needs of a person frequently challenge the store of methods that a counselor can access. There is always a tension, "Have I the skills and the ability to help this person?" In other words, "Will my method be of use to this person in solving his or her problems?" Just as no one counselor can help every counselee, so no one method is suitable for every situation. Certain methods are more useful to apply to one type of problem rather than to another. A strict Freudian is unlikely to be of much use to a person who is seeking spiritual direction, and a person seeking to untangle complex emotional or family issues might be disappointed in what a dyed-in-the-wool behaviorist is able to offer.

Often, too, the problem that the counselor's method first highlights is not always the problem that might best be dealt with first. Adolescents whose family lives are in fragments and who are constantly being shuffled between family members, in and out of state care and the courts, are generally in an emotional mess. To start long-term psycho-emotional counseling with these young people is often a mistake, because the chaos of their physical lives frequently disrupts the counseling process and they end up feeling that they have been abandoned yet again. It is often more helpful that they have a period of certainty and stability in their physical surrounds so that they can rest from the emotional buffeting that they have experienced.

Counselors want to think of themselves as competent. Most of us would like to be able to help everyone who comes to us for assistance. When a counselee comes whose problems lie outside our competency we tend to feel inadequate. We forget our human limitations. Rather than feel inadequate, counselors may deny that their methods will be of little use in a particular instance. Subsequently, when the counseling relationship breaks down and the counselee fails to become more whole and free, we may even blame the counselee for being resistant to treatment

— a resistance which, in this case, would be wholly justified!

We have to recognize that there are some problems which we simply cannot resolve by counseling. We are not helping if we try to counsel the psychopath or people with certain personality disorders. It may be that, as our knowledge increases, we may be able to address these problems in the future, using new counseling methods. It may be that we need to think of alternative ways to help. It may be that there are some people we can never be of help to substantially. Intractable problems threaten counselors who have made their methods a way of life and who have given to their method a value greater than that of a tool. It is always sad when we see someone in need whom we cannot help. It calls for mourning and perhaps prayer, but it does not shake a Christian counselor's sense of self-worth and meaning, nor the counselor's ability to continue the work of liberation in other areas where his or her methods can be of use.

2. Change and the Freedom to Love

There are a variety of goals which various methods claim to achieve, from something as broad as "self-fulfillment" through to specific goals, such as removal of various phobias. Not all are consistent with eliciting greater freedom to love. The vocational guidance counselor, who sees his/her work in terms of increasing competitiveness and matching counselees to the most highly paid jobs, does not necessarily promote greater freedom to love in the counselee. Similarly, the school counselor who is more concerned to make students "fit" rather than address students' real concerns about the school system also fails.

A more complex problem arises when a method appears to be effective at removing a troubling symptom — say, depression — but on closer examination is found to be interfering with a normal grieving process. In other cases, a symptom might disappear in one family member only to occur in another. The good-child/bad-child phenomenon is well known: after a period of counseling, a family announces that their "bad" child is now as good as gold, but his/her model sibling has turned into a little horror. The method used has not, to date, touched the root of the problem. The family is still trapped, even the child who has suddenly become "good."

3. Respect for the Counselee as a Person

With almost all methods, there is a danger that they become simply techniques that treat people as factors in a problem equation. When this happens, counseling may well dehumanize the counselee, the direct opposite of freeing the person to love. Of the various methods on offer, behaviorism poses the greatest risk. The behaviorist counselor tends to pay attention neither to the emotional life of counselees, nor to their understandings of the problem. Indeed, the method eschews insight as not being useful in solving problems. At an extreme, this method posits that people are only a bundle of reactions, for which no freedom is possible. This is not to say that we should discard behaviorism. Behaviorists have well described how we often do act and react, and in many ways they remind us usefully of the limitations of the human condition. However, dogmatic practitioners of the behaviorist method ultimately do not respect persons in their totality, and the method needs to be used with caution.

As a method, the use of categories to describe problems, such as in the psychiatric DSM IV, can be quite useful. It becomes a problem, however, if the people with the conditions become equated with the conditions themselves. Such labeling is often reinforced by bureaucratization in hospitals and the public service where many counselors work.

4. Respect for the Interrelatedness of Reality

If integral liberation is an aim of counseling, then the more levels of interrelatedness that a method can deal with, the more generally successful the method is likely to be. It is not enough for a counselor only to deal with the psychological, or the social, or the spiritual, as though each were a distinct and self-contained entity. Of course, it is at times useful to make distinctions. But the truth is that people are ultimately indivisible and exist in a complex web of relationships.

When we fail to respect the interrelatedness of reality, we often stray into unnecessary blaming and/or inappropriate guilt. I learned this well when I had to deal with adolescents who were stealing. While the adolescents were seen only individually, they tended to be viewed by the family as bad, and subsequently isolated. When I saw the family together, a couple of interesting things occurred. Firstly, I found that one or both of the parents usually had a history of stealing when they were adolescents. Talking about this helped the individual adolescent to feel less deviant, and the family were able to put the current stealing into a context. Secondly, the family began to view stealing as a family issue, and family members started to mobilize to help the adolescent with the stealing problem.

The best methods and the best counselors are open to whatever impinges on the world of the counselee, including issues of development, illness, tragedy, injustice and racism. It is rare indeed for any problem to be solved with straight counseling alone, without reference to other external assistance or change to the external circumstances of the counselee.

5. Effectiveness

Effectiveness is the criteria by which we judge whether we have achieved our goals. The broad aim of Christian counseling, I have argued in this book, is the liberation to love. Within that broad aim, however, there is almost always a number of subsidiary aims: removal of disturbing symptoms; improved interpersonal relationships; increase in assertiveness and so on.

The measure of effectiveness in Christian counseling can cover a number of areas. Firstly, it should be able to show that it has, in fact, achieved its subsidiary aims. Secondly, it should be able to show that it has done this in a manner consistent with the previous four criteria. In sum, we should be able to show that our aims are consistent with the needs of the counselee, that the counselee as a result has achieved greater freedom to love and that we have respected the counselee as a person, as well as his/her interrelatedness to the rest of reality. Finally, we should be able to show that the counseling did bring about changes in the counselee, and that change was not brought about by some other extraneous factor, such as normal development over time.

Many counselors are wary of talk of effectiveness. Some believe that effectiveness cannot be measured because of the subjective and long term nature of change. Certainly, the measurement of effectiveness is neither simple nor easy. However, counselors who do not seek to evaluate results are condemned to forever make the same mistakes and to be ultimately directionless. When we consider the vast amount of counseling that goes on, only a very small percentage of this work is reviewed systematically for effectiveness. Also, much that passes for evaluation is so methodologically flawed as to be useless. Indeed, I believe that the Christian counselor should be taking a lead in this field. Ultimately we have nothing to lose and everything to gain by searching persistently and courageously for the truth: the Truth, as Gutiérrez puts it, that sets us free.

THE CHALLENGE

The method that I have outlined for the Christian counselor in this chapter is challenging. It places the work of the counselor both in the mainstream of developments in counseling in our modern age, and also in the mainstream of the unfolding revelation of God's salvation, the liberation to love. The ability of the Christian counselor to hold together these two positions will be enhanced if the Church, of which the Christian counselor is a member, plays its part in the process of liberation. The role of the Church and its relationship to Christian counselors is the subject of the next chapter.

---

[1] Gutiérrez, Gustavo, "A Discussion of Gustavo Gutiérrez's Work [Lyons, 1985]," in *The Truth Shall Make You Free: Confrontations,* Orbis Books, Maryknoll, New York, 1990, p.5.
[2] id.
[3] ibid., pp.7-8.
[4] Bridgman, Percy, quoted by Mills, C. Wright, *The Sociological Imagination,* Oxford University Press, 1959, Penguin Books, 1970, p.69.
[5] Tutu, Desmond, "Open Letter to Mr. John Vorster," 6 May 1976, in *Hope and Suffering,* Collins Fount Paperback, London, 1983, p.32.

The Church as Sign of Liberation

THE NEED FOR A SIGN

The liberation to love is a long process for the counselee and there are no short cuts. As foreshadowed in the Old Testament, the escape across the Red Sea leads initially into the desert. The meeting with God in the desert does not lead immediately to the promised land, and even when a person has finally left the desert for the land of milk and honey, there are still struggles and regressions — perhaps further exiles.

The liberation to love occurs in the counselee's actual life, not in some idealized, spiritualized or psychic world. In this real world of day to day activity, there is a need for a sign that liberation is possible. The counselor provides one such sign by his or her willingness to provide ongoing "compassion, steadfast love and faithfulness."[1] The counselor offers a sign of hope in what can seem to the counselee a hopeless and desperate world. However, as every counselor knows, this offer and capacity is limited. The counselor is only one person, one hopeful sign in a crowd of negatives. No matter how skilful the counselor, his or her ability is limited. Counselors are fragile human beings like everybody else — despite their best efforts, they sometimes fail, are inauthentic, selfish. Are there, then, other signs of hope?

A person who comes from a happy loving family based in a happy stable community sees a world full of signs of hope. Love is experienced as a sign of hope, a sign that all is not bad, all is not self-centered. However, most counselees, and perhaps most people, do not come from happy loving families, nor do they live in happy stable communities. Often, their experience of the world is just the reverse, or at best ambivalent. The signs they see are mixed messages of hope and despair.

THE CHURCH AS SIGN

One sign is not ambivalent. The church is a sign of hope pointing directly to the liberation to love. Its purpose is to signal to the world that it is God's will and God's providential plan that all should be free to love, that all should be freed from self-centeredness.

The church is a sign of hope because it is first and foremost the body of Christ. (Eph 1:23; 5:30; Col 1:18; 24) The church carries forward the liberation initiated by Christ. The church announces, as does Christ, that the Kingdom of God is upon us, that the liberation of love is not only possible, but already occurring. Hence, Gutiérrez can talk of the church as the "universal sacrament of salvation."[2] The church is a universal sign, one meant to declare to everyone that Christ is come to save and to liberate. Christians are called to unite themselves to this body, with Christ as head and they as parts, to continue the work of liberation. So close is the work of Christ and Christians in the church that St. Paul can say, "It makes me happy to suffer for you, as I am suffering now, and in my own body to do what I can to make up all that has still to be undergone by Christ for the sake of his body, the Church." (Col 1:24)

However, it is apparent to even the most optimistic observer that the institutional church often falls short of its task to be a sign of liberation and a universal sacrament of salvation. Too often, sadly, the church has become a source of oppression and cut itself off from the Body of Christ, with neither meaning nor life. Like a branch cut off from a vine, it withers and dies. (Jn 15:6) At other times, the church seems to become so concerned with its own importance that it forgets that it is a *sign* of salvation, and imagines that it is the fullness of salvation itself. But God is liberating the whole world, not just the church. Denis Edwards advises that, "A local church . . . has to learn to listen to where the liberating God is already at work at the heart of everyday life."[3] The message of liberation is not something that the church can keep exclusively for itself. It is a fallacy to believe, as many Catholics did in the Middle Ages and as many fundamentalists do today, that "there is no salvation outside the church." Such a belief turns Christ's message of universal liberation into a comforting myth for the few. It limits God's action to the church, and it implies that God does not speak to and through the world.

Counselees challenge the church. Poor and trapped as they are, they ask for a sign of liberation. They ask, "Does all this suffering and struggle have meaning? Will I ever be free? What does the society in which I can be free look like?" The church's response to the counselee has to go beyond muttered platitudes and pious teachings. As a sacrament of salvation, the church is obligated to "manifest in its visible structures the message that it bears,"[4] demonstrating that in its service to the world it exercises a preferential option for the poor; that in its communal life it celebrates the coming of the Kingdom; that it listens ever attentively to the liberating word of God; that as a community at prayer it praises, laments and engages in the life and sufferings of God the creator and liberator; that it acts both as counselor and counselee and that in its sacramental life it acts as a sign of liberation for counselees.

SIGNS: 1. The Preferential Option for the Poor

That the church should have a preferential option for the poor is based in the belief that Christ, both in his teaching — particularly in the beatitudes (Mt 5:3; Lk 6:20) — and in his life (2 Cor 8:9), adopted such a preference. Christ is concerned that all should be liberated; especially those most in need of liberation, those incapable of escaping by their own strength. All of us need this liberation, this salvation, but not all of us are aware that we are trapped, particularly those who oppress others. Christ spoke harshly about those whose oppression masqueraded as religious fervor. (Luke 11:37-54; Mt 23)

The preferential option for the poor upsets many of the profit and loss, "common sense" notions of society. Christ loves the poor not because they are good, but simply because they are in need of God's love. God's love is freely given and does not have to be earned. When we are poor, we can have no illusion that we have earned God's love. Often the poor are incapable of earning even a subsistence existence, yet God states specifically that the Kingdom of God belongs to the poor: such is God's close identification. (Luke 5:3)

Not all counselees are physically poor, though of course many are. However, all counselees know that they are trapped and in need of assistance to be free. Their realization is often tentative, and clouded by many anxieties, fantasies and delusions. But, in the act of seeking help, counselees reveal their vulnerability to themselves and to others. Indeed, no effective counseling can take place unless they acknowledge some vulnerability and their own poverty. Often, this is a shocking experience. Many people feel out of control. Their image of themselves as strong and self-sufficient is shattered. They may even feel violated, especially if they are from cultures that stress rugged individualism. In entering the world of the counselee, the counselor enters the world of the poor. If the counselee is to be free, the counselor must start from where the counselee is trapped. Entering this world and attempting the work of liberation, Christian counselors participate in the liberating work of Christ. Through their work, the church announces that Christ is now liberating the world, and that this counseling relationship is the sign of that liberation.

The church is, of course, more than any one particular counseling relationship. The wider church has an obligation to acknowledge and encourage individual signs of liberation offered by its members. Church teaching is vitally important, for the church fails in its mission if it either does not send people out to be signs or, in sending them out, fails to explain adequately to them the significance of their mission. Often, church members conceive of their mission only in terms of organizational maintenance. Similarly, other church members devote their lives to the service of the poor and to advocacy for their rights, and yet never conceive of this as a mission of the church. In this latter group are counselors whose work should be especially celebrated by the church, for through their work they help bring about the Kingdom of God. In Chapter Six I discussed the importance of counselors working in the child abuse field. Equally, I could have discussed the importance of counselors working with the victims of AIDs; with indigenous people in their struggle for justice; with the mentally ill or with the homeless, to name but a fraction of the important fields in which counselors are involved. They are at the cutting edge of God's reality, and if the church is not celebrating liberation to the poor in terms of freedom from injustice; in terms of freedom as human persons; and in terms of freedom to love God and to enter the loving community of the church, then the church is failing in its mission. It is a dead branch cut off from the living Body of Christ that is active in the world.

The ways that individual churches encourage and celebrate their members' works of liberation vary. What is important is that the church culture of liberation center on the belief that both the Kingdom of God and the church as Body of Christ identify radically with the poor.

2. Community: An essential sign

A liberation culture cannot exist without community. Without community, the church is no more than a social institution, little different from many others. Community is the means by which Christians relate to the incarnate Christ. Without community, Christians cannot identify with a Christ who is present in the here and now. Without community, the image of God is a distant historical figure of the first century, or a disembodied spirit that intones injunctions from afar. Community brings God into the here and now or, put another way, God constantly self-reveals through community. It is God's intention that the church be a community, modeled on the Trinity which is the preeminent community of love. As the Spirit of God is present in the center of the community of the Trinity, so too is the Spirit of God present in the center of the community of the church.

3. The Eucharist as Sign

The sacrament of the Eucharist points to the unity of community in Christ. God is present in the breaking of the bread and the sharing of the cup, the most powerful sign of God's inclusive love for the world. However, this sign is often so spiritualized that it points in the wrong direction — to the clouds rather than to God's real presence in the center of the community. It can become a sign of division amongst people who are otherwise united: dividing married couples from each other, dividing people of different religious denominations and, most seriously, excluding many who are most aware of their sinfulness, the very group whom God came to call into community. No wonder, then, that this sign of unity has little appeal for many counselees. Rather than signifying a liberation from disunity, it too often mirrors the counselees' own fragmentation, or offers just another illusion. A church which is serious about serving its counselees must ensure that the sign of the Eucharist is pointing in the right direction, so that counselees can see clearly a sign of unity.

The principal reason that the sign of the Eucharist can point in the wrong direction is that there is often no community to point to, only a group of complacent individuals. Liturgical tricks will not solve the problem when what is needed is a conversion of the church itself. The church has to come to face the difficult fact that structures of evil and sin control communal life, and that the church itself, like the counselee, is in need of liberation. Furthermore, conversion has to be ongoing; the church is the community seeking freedom. All are united in this search. The Eucharist is then a sign that freedom is possible and, indeed, already present, because the Eucharist announces that the Kingdom of God is both present and yet to come.

When a congregation fails to be open to community and to the ongoing conversion that this implies, there are a number of consequences. One of the most important is the disturbed development of faith in the congregation, with the familiar tendency for the average developmental level of adults in church congregations not to rise substantially beyond that of an adolescent.[5] There is, too, pressure from society for the church not to go beyond this level. From society's perspective, this level (the synthetic-conventional level in Fowler's terminology) is a safe level. It offers no substantial threats to the way society currently operates because it is conformist. If a Church tries to move the average developmental level for adults beyond this point, it becomes aware almost immediately how trapped it still is in the structures of sin. Nice, holy, pious, complacent people suddenly turn nasty. The Bishop or Moderator gets letters of complaint; fierce arguments break out in previously placid committees; there are letters to the editor; long-standing pillars of the church walk out in a huff. The church appears to be dying and, indeed a part of it is: the false illusion of a loving community is being destroyed. When this illusion is destroyed a conversion can happen and the church can begin to see afresh the world as God sees it. Then can it see that God is liberating the world and that the church is a sign and not the whole of reality. Conformism becomes a stage, not an end in itself. The continually converting church is open to the God who continually comes afresh to the world. The continually converting church does not worship one image of God, an idol and a false image that claims to be the totality. Rather, it worships a God who is always subject, a God who continually comes and who self-reveals using a multiplicity of often surprising images. Only when the church is undergoing such a conversion can it afford to encourage its members to keep growing through the stages of faith, and to become a community that truly respects diversity.

The continual conversion of churches is especially important for counselees because they are themselves changing. If counseling is successful, counselees may find themselves alienated from a church which is still locked into their previous developmental level, and the church becomes just another source of oppression from which counselees now know they need to be liberated.

4. Scripture as Sign

Integral to the ongoing conversion of the church is its relationship to the liberating word found in the scriptures. Liberation requires considerably more than reading the scriptures. Rather, as Gutiérrez puts it succinctly, scripture "reads us."[6] For the Christian community:

> The word of God is something alive and active: it cuts like a double edged sword but more finely: it can slip through the place where the soul is divided from the spirit, or joints from the marrow; it can judge the secret emotions and thoughts. No created thing can hide from him; everything is uncovered and open to the eyes of the one to whom we must give account of ourselves. (He 4:12-13)

It is, too, a circular process. The church reads the word of God, and the word of God reads the church. It is in this latter reading that the church is called to conversion, as the word of God sees in the depths of the church the hidden structures of evil that inhibit the processes of liberation and salvation.

In this sense, the word of God becomes the counselor of the church. The reading of scripture, not just a cognitive or intellectual activity, is an ongoing, loving dialog between God and people, expressed most beautifully in the Song of Songs with its loving, intimate, sensuous, emotion-charged passages. In scripture, the word of God announces God's love for the world. Hearing this word, the church is called to respond to the love of God, and, in responding, the church realizes its inability to love. It realizes its entrapment and its need for salvation. God as counselor leads the beloved, the world and the church as its witness, into an ever deepening love relationship, as the various shackles of evil fall away.

5. Prayer as Sign.

Prayer is our primary response to God's freely given love, and this is why it is so often said that thankfulness is the heart of prayer. Prayer is an exclamation of joy for God-given liberation. Such prayer speaks from the counselee's central experience of liberation. The counselee knows not only the exhilaration of liberation, but the full range of experiences that come with the struggle to be free, and the effort to remain free, in the face of often fierce opposition. The prayer of the church needs to reflect these realities, if counselees are to make the prayer of the church their own. The Psalms have had a central place in the prayer life of the church, because they speak of life as it is. Sometimes this is too much for pious Christians who are scandalized if the God of the Psalms seems too close, too concerned with the everyday. And it is true — the psalmists address

God at times in a most direct and unholy manner. Like Job, the psalmists may be unhappy with the actions of God, and tell God so directly, yet at the same time affirm their faithfulness to God. As Gutiérrez has pointed out in his discussion of Job, this way of speaking about God is affirmed by God as truthful, and indeed a way of speaking that leads to an even deeper relationship of love, whereas the attitude of the more pious friends of Job is condemned. (Job 42:7)[7]

Prayer can lead to conversion when it leads to a deeper identification with the poor and with all who suffer. Shaken out of complacency, the sufferer realizes that he or she is not the only one who suffers, and the experience is not unique. There are others who suffer as badly and, in many cases, worse. The realization that God loves us in our suffering leads us to acknowledge others in their suffering. That God became a human like us takes on new meaning. God comes not only for me individually but for every person, because God identifies with every person and God suffers in every person. God desires that every person be free. The one who calls out to God honestly in their suffering learns that:

> God has a preferential love for the poor not because they are necessarily better than others, morally or religiously, but simply because they are poor and living in an inhuman situation that is contrary to God's will. The ultimate basis for the privileged position of the poor is not in the poor themselves but in God, in the gratuitousness and universality of God's agapeic love.[8]

THE CHURCH AS COUNSELOR AND COUNSELEE

In Chapter Two I discussed the Christian belief that God is the ultimate counselor. It follows that the church and its members could well see themselves as counselees of God. It is God who liberates, and the church and its members are in constant, ongoing need of liberation. At no time does the church become autonomous of God. Indeed, as we have seen, the church is the Body of Christ.

Our dependence on God as counselor is crucial if we, as either church or member, are to take on the role of counselor. As counselees of God, we set up no false distinctions between counselor and counselee, because we know that we all share the neediness of counselees. To say that I am not a counselee is to say that I am not in need of God's counsel, and that I am not in need of God's liberation or salvation. Implicitly, I would be indicating that I had no need of God and was not a member of God's church. To say that all Christians are counselees flies in the face of that cherished individualism, within the church and without, that suspects that the resort to the use of human counselors is unacceptable human weakness. To believe that we are counselees of God, while at the same time claiming that we are never in need of a human counselor, is to set up a false distinction and to unduly spiritualize God's action. God acts in and through the world. The actions of human counselors, where they are directed toward freedom, participate in the liberating counsel of God. Rather than shun or condemn the work of human counselors, the Christian should be constantly open to the word of God that comes through them. In fact, the wisdom available from a multiplicity of counselors should be part and parcel of every Christian's life. As the Book of Proverbs points out, "where counselors are many, plans succeed," (Prv 15:22) and also "safety lies in many advisors." (Prv 11:14) Only when the church and its members understand the role of counselee can they effectively take up the role of counselor.

Counseling is one of the ways in which the church acts

as a sign of liberation and universal sacrament of salvation. When the church's counsel is directed beyond the confines of the church to the whole human race, the role of counselor often becomes an uncomfortable one, for the world is a reluctant counselee. Not only does creative engagement with the world take great skill, but there are many powerful people and institutions who would prefer to negate the church's counseling role, or confine it to spiritual matters and issues of personal morality. In Australia, a leading counselor of this kind has been Archbishop Peter Hollingsworth, initially as spokesperson for the Brotherhood of St. Laurence, and more lately as Anglican Archbishop of Brisbane. Archbishop Hollingsworth does not issue his counsel from afar, but in solidarity with those who suffer in our society. He has entered into a loving yet challenging dialogue with the Australian Government over issues of justice. More recently, the Australian Catholic Bishops, too, have sought to set up such a dialogue through their statement, *Common Wealth for the Common Good*,[9] and through the ensuing public discussion of the distribution of wealth in Australia.

Individual Christian counselors, through their work, participate in the wider counseling of the church. There is no Christian counseling outside this work of the church. In this context, pastoral counseling is a subset of a wider class of counseling that I have here called Christian counseling. The distinction between pastoral counseling and other types of counseling is not valid if it implies that counseling by Christians, which does not carry the label "pastoral" or belong to that tradition, is not equally a function of the church's liberating work in society.

RECOGNIZING THE ROLE OF COUNSELOR WITHIN THE CHURCH

If the world is in need of counsel and each Christian a

counselee, there is a substantial need for Christian counselors. For the church to respond to this need, we must first recognize the role as an important one within the life of the church and support it with our prayer and, in some cases, by ordination. At present, ordination is often restricted to priests and pastors. But, rather than point to liberation, ordination often points to an entrenched male hierarchical power structure within the church, a misuse of a sacrament. It would be far more liberating if ordination were used whenever a church, guided by the Spirit, embarked on an undertaking and sent forth members to achieve that undertaking. The laying on of hands, which is the basic symbol of this sacrament, is a powerful sign of the interrelatedness of the community of faith. The counselor is not alone, but is both commissioned and supported by the community acting as the Body of Christ. The ordained counselor would then be acknowledged as one minister, amongst many, charged with the spreading of the good news of God's liberation to the world.

Furthermore, if we are to take the church's counseling role seriously, we need to facilitate training for counselors at a variety of levels, depending on the needs of the time and our discernment of God's providential will. Some people are natural counselors, but nearly everyone can benefit from training. Often major problems can be averted when people have simple communication skills that allow them to communicate empathy rather than emotionless advice. Perhaps churches appear so unfriendly because their people lack these basic skills. If a church is to become a community, it needs not only counselees but also counselors. Similarly, those involved in counseling to the world need backup training and support. No counseling is easy, but this type of counseling is perhaps one of the most difficult, because of the fierce resistance often offered by the world.

THE COUNSELEE AND SIGNS OF GRACE

Freedom and forgiveness of sin go together, and counselors often witness reconciliations when people are freed from the evil that previously has trapped them. Such moments are signs of even greater things to come, of an even freer, more loving existence in the future. Some churches call reconciliation a sacrament for this reason, for in it they see the liberating presence of God. Unfortunately, these same churches can restrict the word "sacrament" to what happens between a hierarchical minister and a member of the congregation. If reconciliation and the forgiveness of sin is indeed a sacrament, then the church would be wise to acknowledge it whenever and wherever it occurs. The church as sacrament of salvation cannot ignore the unfolding of God's forgiveness in the world.

Neither can the church afford to ignore the action of God in the experience of conversion, usually acknowledged in the sacrament of Baptism and, to some degree, in the sacrament of Confirmation. Yet often these sacraments, too, become unduly spiritualized, too detached from everyday experience. This is particularly a problem with infant Baptism. There is a place for infant Baptism for, as I have shown earlier, it is possible for a person to participate in the experience of conversion of a forbear. While it is impossible for an infant to understand the significance of a Baptism, families and communities are capable of understanding its significance. For this reason Baptism should be a time of reflecting on the significance of the Baptism experience that the child is entering — not in vague generalities but, rather, as a specific historical remembering of the conversion experience of the child's family, including key conversions to Christianity, if they can be remembered, as well as conversions that have occurred since that time. The service can offer opportunities for remembering also the conversion experience of the church community that the child is entering, including both the scriptural record and the conversion events in the church's more recent history.

The Confirmation sacrament could also signal for the Christian his or her continuing conversion. Just as conversion is not a once in a life time event, nor need Confirmation be a once only event, but instead could be linked to something like Fowler's stages of faith. Each stage does not necessarily represent a conversion but, for each stage to unfold, there needs to be a conversion in the life of the person. The use of the sacrament to mark these stages would further legitimize and encourage change in the life of the counselee.

While these changes to the sacrament of Confirmation may seem radical, a similar change has occurred within the Catholic church in the understanding of the sacrament now called the Anointing of the Sick, and previously called Extreme Unction. Previously this sacrament was only administered when a person was thought to be about to die. Now the sacrament is used frequently, often on a monthly basis in a communal setting, to signify God's care and healing of the sick, and God's presence with them. This change has been widely welcomed within the Catholic community and the sacrament is now extremely popular, whereas previously it was viewed with fear as the sacrament of the last gasp. Such a change also has advantages to counselees who feel free to use the Sacrament as a sign of God's healing power.

Individual sacraments, important as they are, do not exist or have potency in isolation. They are not magical phenomena. Individual sacraments derive their meaning from the basic sacrament of the church, and the church, in turn, derives its meaning from its mission. We, as church, are sent out by Christ to announce the good news of liberation and salvation to the world. In so doing, the church does the will of the Father, and participates in the work of the Son and in the power of the Holy Spirit, as well as in the love of the Trinity. The good news of salvation is both the message and the person of Christ, but not a salvation that can simply be tacked onto life. Rather, it is salvation in the midst of life. It is love radically realized, incarnate in history, in the relationship between Christ and his people and the Father, in the mystery of the Spirit.

COUNSELING AND GOD'S UNFOLDING LOVE

In this book I have attempted to show that the Christian counselor has a vital role to play in the unfolding self-revelation of God's love. The Christian counselor is a sacrament of liberation and therefore participates in the universal sacrament of salvation which is the church. In order to perform this responsibility fully, the counselor must forgo the complacency of a self-contained, inward-looking and self-satisfied church culture. Rather, the Christian counselor challenges the church to join realistically with each counselee in his/her struggle to be free to love. The loving identification with the counselee mirrors the identification of Christ with the poor. I have not argued for professional counselors, but for the whole church community to respond to the challenge to be open to the liberating word that is being spoken through the counselee. Only when we in the church are fully open to this word can we say that the Kingdom of God is upon us, and can we say with Christ:

>The spirit of the Lord has been given to me,
>for he has anointed me.
>He has sent me to bring the good news to the poor,
>to proclaim liberty to captives
>and to the blind new sight,
>to set the downtrodden free,
>to proclaim the Lord's year of favor.

(Luke 4:18-19)

[1] Morgan, Oliver J., "Elements in a Spirituality of Pastoral Care," *The Journal of Pastoral Care,* 1989, Vol.43, No.2, p.102.
[2] Gutiérrez, Gustavo, *A Theology of Liberation,* Orbis Books, Maryknoll, New York, 1973, pp.252-262.
[3] Edwards, Denis, *Called to be Church in Australia: An Approach to the Renewal of Local Churches,* St. Paul Publications, Homebush, 1989, p.38.
[58] Gutiérrez, op.cit., p.261.
[59] Fowler, James, *Stages of Faith: The Psychology of Human Development and the Quest for Meaning,* Collins Dove, Blackburn, 1981, p.294.
[60] Gutiérrez, Gustavo, *The Truth Shall Make You Free: Confrontations,* Orbis Books, Maryknoll, New York, 1990, p.47.
[61] Gutiérrez, Gustavo, *On Job, God-Talk and the Suffering of the Innocent,* Orbis Books, Maryknoll, New York, 1987, p.11 and pp.82-92.
[9] Australian Catholic Bishops' Conference, *Common Wealth for the Common Good,* Collins Dove, Blackburn, 1992.

Index

A
aggression 47
AIDs 32, 101
alcohol 8, 32, 61
Anointing of the Sick 111
apartheid 38
Augustine, St. 24
Auschwitz 30, 54, 70
Australia 108

B
Baptism 110
Baum, Gregory 35, 36, 48
behaviorism 89, 90, 92
Betts, Donni 42, 49
Betts, George 42, 43, 49
Birch, Charles 49
Blake, William 78
Body of Christ 12, 98, 107, 109
Bridgman, Percy 95
Buddha 39
bureaucratization of counseling 7, 92

C
Catholic 26, 36, 46, 99, 108, 111
change 5, 23, 27, 58–60, 62, 68, 69, 73–4, 77, 80, 88, 91–2, 111
Chardin Tielhard de 56
child abuse 8, 30, 57, 65–81, 86, 101
church 97–113
Common Wealth for the Common Good 108
communion 20, 26–8
community 52, 58, 83, 97, 99, 101–4
compassion 23, 74–7
Confirmation 110–11
conversion 20, 51–62, 66–9, 77–80, 103–6, 110–11,
counseling techniques 4, 5, 32, 34, 89
crucifixion 33
culture 6–9, 24–5, 59, 68, 100, 101

D
Darwin, Charles 55
death 32–3, 70, 75
deceit 33, 68

despair 43, 73, 75, 98
Deutero-Isaiah 15
Divine will 11–21, 36, 47, 52, 73, 87, 88, 98, 109
Droegemueller, William 80
drugs 8, 32, 61
DSM IV 92

E
Edwards, Denis 99, 113
effectiveness 48, 89, 93–4
Ellul, Jacques 25, 34
empathy 7, 75–6, 109
Erikson, Erik 39
Eucharist 101–4
evil 27, 38, 67–74, 76–8, 80, 103, 105
exodus 87

F
faith development 4, 39–46, 48
feminism 38
forgiveness 29–30, 110
Fowler, James W. 36, 39–46, 58–9, 63, 103, 111, 113
Freud, Anna 34
Freud, Sigmund 6
Freudian theory 55, 89, 90
fundamentalism 38, 99

G
Gilligan, Carole 31, 34
Goldstein, Joseph 34
grace 27, 69–74, 79, 110–12
Greenwood, Ernest 7, 9
Gutiérrez, Gustavo 5, 25–8, 34, 54, 57, 62, 67, 81–5, 94–5, 98, 104, 106, 113

H
Hannaford, John 49
Hart, Thomas 23, 34
Hauerwas, Stanley 34
history 7, 11, 12, 27, 112
Hollingsworth, Archbishop Peter 108
homeless 101
hope 8, 40, 69–75, 77, 97–8
Hulme, William E. 3, 9

I

ideology 51, 56
Images of God 12–19, 35–48, 54, 61–2, 102, 104
indigenous people 8, 30, 101
injustice 13, 26, 30, 33, 38, 52, 71, 73, 93, 101
International Society for the Prevention of Child Abuse and Neglect 73, 78
Isaiah 13

J

Job 15, 106
Johnson, Elizabeth A. 49
Jung, Carl 6
justice 30–1; *see also* injustice
juvenile delinquency 31

K

Kelly, Tony 49
Kempe, C. Henry 77, 81
Kennedy, Michael J. 9
Kingdom of God 53–4, 57, 63, 72, 79–80, 98, 101, 103, 112
Kohlberg, L. 31, 34, 39

L

Lewin, Kurt 56
Libertatis Conscientia 26
Lonergan, Bernard 58–60, 63, 76
Lynch, Margaret 73, 80

M

Marx, Karl 55–6, 84
McFague, Sallie 37, 49
meaninglessness 32
mentally ill 87, 101
mercy 30–1
methods of counseling 83–95
Mills, C. Wright 95
Minuchin, Salvador 34
mission 101, 111
Morgan, Oliver J. 23, 32, 34, 113
Moses 14, 35, 70

O

omnipotent 38, 49
Ordination 3, 4, 109

P

Ormerod, Neil 9, 72, 81

parenting 31, 61
pastoral counselor 3–5, 7, 108
pathos 75–6
Paul, St. 17, 19, 61, 71, 98
Piaget, Jean 6, 39
prayer 52, 87–8, 99, 105–6, 109
preferential option for the poor 99–101
professionalization 7–8
projection 68–9
prophet 9, 14, 17

R

reconciliation 30, 110
righteousness 13, 45

S

sacrament 23, 44, 98–9, 102, 108–12
salvation 12, 26, 95, 98–9, 105, 107–8, 110, 112
Scripture 11–21, 35–6, 47, 52, 104–5
self-deception 33
self-esteem 29, 77
Silver, Henry K. 81
Silverman, Frederic N. 81
sin, *see* evil
Skinner, B F 6
Solnit, Albert J. 34
Sophia 39
Steele, Brandt F. 81
Stockton, Eugene D. 49
suffering 29–30, 33, 36, 38, 45, 47, 61, 67, 72–3, 75, 85, 98–9, 106

T

"The Battered-Child Syndrome" 78
Thornhill, John 49
truth 25, 33, 44, 56, 94
Tutu, Archbishop Desmond 74–6, 86, 95

U

unemployment 8, 26, 86

V

Vaughan, Richard 3–4, 9
Vittachi, Anuradha 74, 81

W

Winnicott, Donald W. 34
wisdom 8, 12, 14, 17, 39, 107